The Blessed Life Bible Study

Claiming God's Blessings Every Day

Blessed

BERAKAH

בְּרָכָה

www.TheBlessedLifeBook.com

Library of Congress Cataloging-in-Publication Data is
available.
ISBN 978-0-9987903-2-9
ISBN 978-0-9987903-3-6 (ebook)

Printed in the United States of America

1

"Blessing" defined

God's favor or protection[1]

Numbers 6:24-26
The Message Bible

God bless you and keep you,
God smile on you and gift you,
God look you full in the face
and make you prosper.

A Prayer of Blessing based on Numbers 6

May the Lord Bless You and Keep You,
Make His Face to Shine Upon You
And Be Gracious Unto You.
May the Lord Lift Up His Countenance Upon You
And Give You Peace.
AMEN

---

[1] "Blessings." BibleStudyTools.com
http://www.biblestudytools.com/topical-verses/bible-verses-about-blessings/
(accessed February 28, 2017).

Table of Contents

INTRODUCTION

How To Use This Bible Study

We all want to live *The Blessed Life*. We long for a life filled with happiness and joy without end. Blessings can come to us in the form of material possessions, physical health, emotional stability, and being spiritually grounded. While each person's journey to blessing may be different, there is one commonality in all lasting blessings in our life: our relationship with God in Christ Jesus.

The purpose of this Bible study is to show you the path to *The Blessed Life*. I ask that you have an open mind and heart to hear the Holy Spirit speak to you as you work through this study; explore the practical foundations for how to create a continual flow of blessings in your life.

I live my life on a foundation of God's blessings. Just before I sign my name to letters and memos, I use the salutation of "Blessings". I believe that God has blessed me incredibly. Many of my greatest blessings have come as I travel through times of personal growth and sometimes pain. As a pastor, I listen often to the struggles and pain of others. My calling as a pastor is to point others to the fountain of blessings that God stands ready to give. As a Sociology major, I know a great deal about the dysfunction of our world. Our world would be very different if we as humans focused more on the blessings of life, rather than that which degrades and tears down.

Blessings are a part of life. Think about the analogy of lifting weights. Lifting weights tears down the muscle, much like life can wear on us and tear us down. If we lift weights without rest, we eventually will collapse under the pressure of fatigue, exhaustion, or physical breakdown. Our bodies need rest in order to recover and replenish. Finding blessings is like the rest we need to recover from lifting weights. As we continually repeat the

5

process of working out, resting, working out, and resting, eventually our bodies recover and become physically healthy. The process is not fun, but the end result is a physically fit us. Life is hard. It can leave us without hope and demoralized. But if we look around us, there is always a blessing to be found … many times in the midst of the storm. As we find blessings around us, it allows God to build us up so that we can weather the storm. We come out on the other side of the storm stronger than ever before, and ready to face what life sends our way.

Not all circumstances that come our way are bad. Many life events are great and make us exceedingly happy. The challenge for us is to recognize blessings when they come so that we can enjoy life and reach even higher mountain tops of joy and happiness than we ever thought possible. Recognizing blessings (spiritual, physical, and emotional blessings) allows us to "bank" our blessings for a rainy day. Those "banked" blessings help us to keep our hope and to remain resolute even when we walk through the valleys of life.

The Ideal Way to Study

Read the content and answer the questions BEFORE each Bible study session. It will make your session time more rich as you can spend the bulk of your time discussing instead of reading the material.

The Book is Divided Into Four Sections

In Section One, we answer the question, "What is *The Blessed Life?*" Blessings are found throughout the Bible. We learn from the covenant blessing God formed with Moses. We discuss adversity and how we navigate the good and bad times of life to find blessings on each step of our journey. Questions will be discussed like, "What does it mean to be prosperous?" and "How can we be blessed even more?"

Section Two recognizes the need to be lifelong learners, learning from the successes and mistakes of others. Four sets of people will be discussed. Given my Wesleyan roots, we begin with John Wesley. I believe that Wesley is a great example of someone who experienced the valleys of life and turned his life into a blessing that extended beyond his lifetime. The denominations that came out of his ministry are prime examples of generational blessings begun by Wesley that continue to give into the present day. After Wesley, we discuss Billy Graham. Graham is one of the most blessed Christians of all time. Like Wesley, he started many of the generational blessings that continue to bless the Christian Church into the present day. He is unique because his influence was worldwide. He preached crusades in countries that were hostile to Christianity, and yet people by the millions were receptive to receiving Jesus Christ. The latter part of Section Two centers on The Church Fathers, both ancient and recent. There is a lot we can learn from the fathers of our faith who risked their lives to ensure that the message of Christianity would be prosperous for all time.

In Section Three, practical ways are given to bless others. How can we be blessed in our marriage? What are some of the ways we can make sure that our children are blessed and live a joyful life? We answer these questions and more as we give you easy ways that you can value your marriage and your children. I offer you one tip that will allow you to bless others over the long term: Be a note writer. Value snail mail and continue to drop notes to others with positive messages from time to time. It will strengthen your relationships with others as they start to view you as one who cares about them.

Section Four contains a challenge. I challenge you to begin living *The Blessed Life* today, no matter your current age or life circumstance. Change what you can in your life by the power of the Holy Spirit. Honor the spiritual gifts God has given you. It all starts with knowing Jesus Christ as your personal Lord and Savior.

My promise to you is this: If you apply *The Blessed Life* principles, you will see an exponential increase in blessings for you and others around you. You will become someone that experiences blessings right now and who blesses others. I make this promise to you not because I am a miracle worker, but because

I know what *The Blessed Life* looks like in my own life. My only regret is that I did not begin to live out *The Blessed Life* sooner!

God Bless you and know that I am praying for you by name as you work through this Bible study. For more on *The Blessed Life*, including additional resources to assist you in living *The Blessed Life*, visit http://www.theblessedlifebook.com.

SECTION ONE

What is The Blessed Life?

SESSION ONE
Covenant Blessings Between God and Us

OPEN THE BIBLE STUDY SESSION WITH PRAYER. ASK GOD TO BLESS YOUR TIME TOGETHER.

ANSWER THE QUESTIONS FOR GROUP DISCUSSION BELOW:

Deutoronic Blessing from God

Deuteronomy 28:1-6 (NIV)- If you fully obey the Lord your God and carefully follow all his commands I give you today, the Lord your God will set you high above all the nations on earth. All these blessings will come on you and accompany you if you obey the Lord your God: You will be blessed in the city and blessed in the country. The fruit of your womb will be blessed, and the crops of your land and the young of your livestock—the calves of your herds and the lambs of your flocks. Your basket and your kneading trough will be blessed. You will be blessed when you come in and blessed when you go out.

John Wesley's Covenant Prayer:

I am no longer my own, but thine.
Put me to what thou wilt, rank me with whom thou wilt.
Put me to doing, put me to suffering.
Let me be employed for thee or laid aside for thee,
exalted for thee or brought low for thee.
Let me be full, let me be empty.
Let me have all things, let me have nothing.
I freely and heartily yield all things to thy pleasure and disposal.
And now, O glorious and blessed God, Father, Son and Holy Spirit,
thou art mine, and I am thine.
So be it.

10

And the covenant which I have made on earth,
let it be ratified in heaven.
Amen.[2]

The *Blessed Life* book discusses in detail the covenants of God with Abraham and Noah. In Session One of *The Blessed Life Bible Study*, we will take a deeper dive into the covenant of God with Moses. We will evaluate how obedience to the Ten Commandments creates the conditions in which blessings can thrive.

The blessings that come from being obedient to the will of God are called *covenant blessings*. Covenant blessings are active blessings. God lays out the plan of blessing that He has for humanity. He then waits to see if humanity will respond by surrendering to His perfect and pleasing will. When humanity follows God's will, blessings always follow. When humanity resists God's will, we miss His blessing.

Think about it like this. I remember driving down the interstate in New Orleans just after Hurricane Katrina. We allowed GPS to be our guide. We had a map, but thought GPS could not be wrong! The map was ready to take us to the church where we would do our mission work. GPS took us to a ferry yard where the ferry was not running. We backtracked several miles to turn around. Not only did we lose time and get frustrated, but our food was cold when we arrived at our check-in center. The situation would have turned out much differently if we had followed the map. God's perfect and pleasing will is the road map. We follow his perfect and pleasing will to find blessings.

The Covenant of God with Moses

Background

In Genesis 32, God changes Jacob's name to "Israel." In Hebrew, the name Israel means "God will prevail," and it is used to signify that Jacob wrestled with God, but God still ultimately

---

[2] Book of Offices of the British Methodist Church, 1936

prevailed. Jacob's twelve sons became the basis for the twelve tribes of Israel.

Joseph was one of the twelve sons of Jacob. While we could spend an entire study on Joseph, the most important detail is that through a series of events (his brothers throwing him into a pit and eventually selling him into slavery), Joseph received God's blessing as he became the Vizier of Egypt, the highest ranking servant who under Pharaoh. During the seven years of abundance, Joseph ordered some of the harvest to be stored up in Egypt . A severe famine followed in Egypt and the surrounding countries. During this time, his eleven brothers came from Canaan (modern day Israel) to ask Joseph for food. He invited his eleven brothers, their father, and their families to live in Egypt during the famine.

After the death of Joseph, the Israelites became slaves when a successor Pharaoh did not have favor for Joseph and his descendents. Pharaoh cast the Israelites into persecution and harsh work conditions, creating the need for God to send someone who would redeem the Israelites and bring them back from Egypt into the Promised Land of Canaan.

Exodus 1:8-14 (NIV) says, "Then a new king, to whom Joseph meant nothing, came to power in Egypt. "Look," he said to his people, "the Israelites have become far too numerous for us. Come, we must deal shrewdly with them or they will become even more numerous and, if war breaks out, will join our enemies, fight against us and leave the country." So they put slave masters over them to oppress them with forced labor, and they built Pithom and Rameses as store cities for Pharaoh. But the more they were oppressed, the more they multiplied and spread; so the Egyptians came to dread the Israelites and worked them ruthlessly. They made their lives bitter with harsh labor in brick and mortar and with all kinds of work in the fields; in all their harsh labor the Egyptians worked them ruthlessly."

ENTER MOSES

Exodus 2:24 tells us, "God heard their groaning and he remembered His covenant with Abraham, with Isaac and with Jacob. So God looked on the Israelites and was concerned about them."

At first, Moses did not want the job. He made excuses before God. They included Moses' belief that he lacked the ability to speak well. So, God gave Moses Aaron, his brother, to be the one who spoke. Through much heartache and ten plagues, the people were delivered out "of Egypt with great power and a mighty hand." (Exodus 32:11, NIV) During their forty years of wandering in the wilderness, God made a covenant with the Israelites at Mount Sinai :

> Then Moses went up to God, and the Lord called to him from the mountain and said, "This is what you are to say to the descendants of Jacob and what you are to tell the people of Israel: 'You yourselves have seen what I did to Egypt, and how I carried you on eagles' wings and brought you to myself. Now if you obey me fully and keep my covenant, then out of all nations you will be my treasured possession. Although the whole earth is mine, you will be for me a kingdom of priests and a holy nation.' These are the words you are to speak to the Israelites." (Exodus 19:3-6, NIV)

The people agreed to the covenant. In Exodus 19:8 (NIV), "The people all responded together, "We will do everything the Lord has said." So Moses brought their answer back to the Lord."

What was in the covenant?

The covenant was the Ten Commandments, given by God to Moses to share with the people. It was practical laws that helped the people to live Godly lives. John Wesley called "sanctification" the process through which we become holy or set apart. We must caution that the Mosaic Covenant did not serve to save people from their sins.[3] It served to help people live holy lives so that they could draw closer to God.

---

[3] Barrick, William. "The Mosaic Covenant." The Master's Seminary Journal, Vol. 10, Issue 2, Fall 1999, p. 218.

This context for the Ten Commandments is especially important as we discuss living *The Blessed Life* in terms of covenant relationship with God. The more that we follow the commandments of God and are obedient to His will, the more we will experience His blessings. We are obedient because we want to be blessed. It is a cause and effect relationship.

The Ten Commandments were not permanent. They were not intended by God to be the end all be all of God's instructions to His people. Jeremiah 31:31-34 (NIV) mentions:

"The days are coming," declares the Lord,
    "when I will make a new covenant
with the people of Israel
    and with the people of Judah.
It will not be like the covenant
    I made with their ancestors
when I took them by the hand
    to lead them out of Egypt,
because they broke my covenant,
    though I was a husband to them,"
declares the Lord.
"This is the covenant I will make with the people of Israel
    after that time," declares the Lord.
"I will put my law in their minds
    and write it on their hearts.
I will be their God,
    and they will be my people.
No longer will they teach their neighbor,
    or say to one another, 'Know the Lord,'
because they will all know me,
    from the least of them to the greatest,"
declares the Lord.
"For I will forgive their wickedness
    and will remember their sins no more."

While the covenant God made with Jesus does not nullify the Mosaic covenant, the Israelites' inability to be loyal to the Mosaic covenant created the eventual need for Jesus to

14

come into the world in order for humankind to be redeemed. God's plan all along was for Him to redeem His people and continually draw His people unto Himself. He desired to redeem his people because of His unconditional love for them. That same love is present for us today.

The Ten Commandments are still held in high esteem by Christians today. As such, courthouses historically have displayed the Ten Commandments. Hollywood honored them with the great Charlton Heston movie of long ago. When I was young, we performed the Ten Commandments in a children's musical in my home church. Christianity still honors the Ten Commandments because they continue to help us live out our faith and draw us closer to God.

The Ten Commandments (Exodus 20:1-17, MSG)

Exodus 20: 3 (MSG) - No other gods, only me.

In this modern age, what gods (little "g") do people worship?

_____

_____

_____

How could other gods come before the true God?

_____

_____

_____

How might people profess to worship God and yet have other gods?

_____

_____

_____

What does it mean to love the world? Consider 1 John 2:15-16 and then reply.

_____

_____

_____

Why would friends of the world be enemies of God? Read James 4:4.

_____

_____

_____

Why can't we serve two masters? Read Matthew 6:24 and comment.[4]

_____

_____

_____

---

[4] Questions adapted from The First Commandment- Do Not Worship Other gods. United Church of God (ucg.org) https://www.ucg.org/the-first-commandment-do-not-worship-other-gods (accessed March 17, 2017).

Exodus 20:4-6 (ESV)- No carved gods of any size, shape, or form of anything whatever, whether of things that fly or walk or swim. Don't bow down to them and don't serve them because I am God, your God, and I'm a most jealous God, punishing the children for any sins their parents pass on to them to the third, and yes, even to the fourth generation of those who hate me. But I'm unswervingly loyal to the thousands who love me and keep my commandments.

What idols do we worship instead of God? What parallel passages of Scripture come to mind?

_____

_____

_____

Do we ever worship the church service instead of worshipping the One for whom the church service is intended?

_____

_____

_____

How does God feel about us worshipping anything other than Him?

_____

_____

_____

Does the concept of a generational blessing or curse apply to how we live?

_____

_____

_____

Exodus 20:7 (MSG)- No using the name of God, your God, in curses or silly banter; God won't put up with the irreverent use of his name.

What is our culture's attitude toward the use of God's name? Do the people you come into contact with have a reverence for God's name or do they use His name in vain?

_____

_____

_____

What is your reaction when you hear someone use God's name thoughtlessly or without respect?

_____

_____

_____

What have you learned about using God's name properly and improperly?

_____

_____

_____

Why is obedience to God vital to a positive personal relationship with God and experiencing God's blessings?

_____

_____

_____

Will all people some day show honor to God's name? HINT: Read Psalm 145.[5]

_____

_____

_____

Exodus 20: 8-11- Observe the Sabbath day, to keep it holy. Work six days and do everything you need to do. But the seventh day is a Sabbath to God, your God. Don't do any work—not you, nor your son, nor your daughter, nor your servant, nor your maid, nor your animals, not even the foreign guest visiting in your town. For in six days God made Heaven, Earth, and sea, and everything in them; he rested on the seventh day. Therefore God blessed the Sabbath day; he set it apart as a holy day.

---

[5] Questions adapted from The Third Commandment- Do Not Misuse God's Name. United Church of God (ucg.org)
https://www.ucg.org/teen-bible-study/teen-bible-study-volume-3-ten-commandments/third-comman dment-do-not-misuse-gods-nam (accessed March 17, 2017).

Historically, some Jewish Rabbis estimated that the maximum allowable distance for someone to travel to worship on the Sabbath was 1000-1200 yards (based on Joshua 3:4). If you observed the Sabbath like many early Orthodox Jews, how would your life change? How might this inform some things you are currently doing and help you to observe Sabbath rest more?

_____

_____

_____

Read Luke 13:10-17. How did Jesus show the religious leader's hypocrisy in accusing him of breaking the Sabbath?

_____

_____

_____

Why did the early Christians do so much preaching on the Sabbath (Acts 13:43, 18:4)?

_____

_____

_____

Exodus 20:12 (MSG)- Honor your father and mother so that you'll live a long time in the land that God, your God, is giving you.

How do we honor our father and mother when they are not perfect? (Consider the role of God's unconditional agape love in how we can respond to our parents in a God honoring way.)

_____

_____

_____

How do we stay true to the commandment to honor our father and mother when they are not Christian?

_____

_____

_____

Someone once said that we can choose our friends but we cannot choose our family. As you think about this, how can we stay true to ourselves and who God is calling us to be without severing the relationship with our family, especially in the case of family dysfunction?

_____

_____

_____

How can you take the positive experiences you have enjoyed with your parents and improve upon the negative experiences as you are a father or mother to your own children?

_____

Exodus 20:13-14 (MSG)- No murder and No adultery.

Christians view murder and adultery as "morally unacceptable" around the world. Murder is punished by various means (the death penalty and imprisonment). While adultery may not be a crime, the broken relationships that result from adultery cannot be overstated.

Given adultery's place of importance as one of the Ten Commandments God gave Moses, how can we place safeguards and boundaries in our lives to insure that we do not fall victim to adultery? (See Jeremiah 31:21-25. The message of Jeremiah was primarily intended for the Jews experiencing the Babylonian exile. God allowed them to be conquered because of their sin. But, he also clearly provided a way back along with a promise of prosperity when they returned.)

If we currently find ourselves in an adulterous relationship, what support should we seek to help us stop the affair and begin to repair relationships with others around us?

How do we seek God's forgiveness and strength when an affair occurs? This question is important not only for the persons caught in adultery, but the victims that are affected.

_____

_____

_____

What does the concept of finding "a new normal" mean to you in the aftermath of murder or an affair? (consider Toby Mac's song "Move." You may Google the lyrics.)

_____

_____

_____

Exodus 20:15 (MSG)- No stealing.

Leviticus 19:11 (NIV) says, "Do not steal. Do not lie. Do not deceive one another." How are stealing and lying related?

_____

_____

_____

1 Timothy 6:10 (NIV) says, "For the love of money is a root of all kinds of evil. Some people, eager for money, have wandered from the faith and pierced themselves with many griefs." How does

this verse reconcile with the act of physically or emotionally stealing from someone else?

_____

_____

_____

Exodus 20:16 (MSG)- No lies about your neighbor.

Jesus referred to Satan as "a liar and the father of lies" (John 8:44). By contrast, Jesus declared himself to be the Truth (John 14:6). God himself "does not lie" (Titus 1:2). In his holiness, he is incapable of lying. As the apostle John put it, "God is light; in him there is no darkness at all" (1 John 1:5).[6]

Sarah Sumner defines the *Seven Levels of Lying* as:

1. We tell the lie.
2. We self protect.
3. We develop a habit of lying.
4. We begin to believe the lies we are telling others.
5. We justify our lies as a positive good.
6. We compartmentalize. We tell people what they want and need to hear for us to get ahead.
7. Lying flips duty on its head. It becomes the culture of a family or business to lie. Persons who challenge the norm will be called whistleblowers.[7]

---

[6] Sumner, Sarah. *The Seven Levels of Lying*. Christianity Today. May 11, 2011. Accessed via http://www.christianitytoday.com/ct/2011/may/7-levelslying.html?start=3 on March 18, 2017.
[7] Sumner, Sarah. *The Seven Levels of Lying*.

How do you feel about people who you know are lying but they think you are clueless as to their falsehoods? How would Jesus respond to a lier?

_____

_____

_____

Is lying ever okay? (see Ephesians 4:15)

_____

_____

_____

How can you avoid lying in your own life? (Sarah Sumner goes on to say, "Pastor Bill Hybels once said something to the effect that pastors who journal don't fall. That statement makes sense to me, because journaling is a means of telling oneself the truth. As long as we don't lie to ourselves, we can manage to stay out of Level #4. But in order to stay out of Level #3 and Level #2, we need people to confess to when we lie at Level #1)."[8]

_____

_____

_____

Exodus 20:17 (MSG)- No lusting after your neighbor's house—or wife or servant or maid or ox or donkey. Don't set your heart on anything that is your neighbor's.

---

[8] Sumner, Sarah. *The Seven Levels of Lying.*

In seeking to avoid lust, we must first understand why we lust. There are five major reasons that we lust after something or someone else:

1) Lust is a willful act into which we give.
2) We enjoy it.
3) It brings us instant gratification.
4) We focus our attention in a way that is not right.
5) It often is accompanied by a deep seeded emotional urge we do not fully understand.[9]

What does the Bible say about lust? (see Psalm 101:3, Matthew 5:28, and 1 John 2:16)

_____

_____

_____

How do we differentiate between a God given desire a lust? (see Psalm 139:23-24)

_____

_____

_____

Blessings Are Found in Covenant Relationship with God

Deutoronomy 11:26-28 (NIV) says, "I've brought you today to the crossroads of Blessing and Curse.

---

[9] Vanderpek, Jim. *Understanding Lust*. Christianity Today. http://www.christianitytoday.com/biblestudies/articles/spiritualformation/understanding-lust.html?start=2 (accessed March 18, 2017).

The Blessing: if you listen obediently to the commandments of God, your God, which I command you today.

The Curse: if you don't pay attention to the commandments of God, your God, but leave the road that I command you today, following other gods of which you know nothing.

God bestows upon us a covenant blessing so that as we live in Him and for Him, God can bless us beyond belief!

RECEIVE PRAYER REQUESTS BEFORE JOINING IN UNISON IN THE CLOSING PRAYER:

Dear Lord, thank you for your blessings that you continually bring into my life. Thank you for my trials as I know that I will be victorious over them as I trust in you. Thank you for sending Jesus to die on the cross for my sins. Today, I give you my heart and soul as I commit to live in a covenant relationship with you. Show me how to follow your law, not out of compulsion, but out your great love for me. I claim your covenant blessings as I trust in you from this day forward. In Jesus' name, AMEN.

HOMEWORK: READ SESSION TWO AND WRITE DOWN YOUR ANSWERS TO THE QUESTIONS FOR GROUP DISCUSSION BEFORE THE NEXT GROUP SESSION

www.TheBlessedLifeBook.com

SESSION TWO
Blessings Through Adversity

OPEN THE BIBLE STUDY SESSION WITH PRAYER. ASK GOD TO BLESS YOUR TIME TOGETHER.

ANSWER THE QUESTIONS FOR GROUP DISCUSSION BELOW:

Blessings should not depend upon how good or how bad situations currently are in our lives. Consider if someone simultaneously had his home foreclosed on but also received word that his child was okay after a serious scare. Surely he would say that he is blessed even though he feels conflicted about something good and something bad coming into his life at the same time. Consider also how the Apostle Paul must have felt while, in prison, he ministered to the lifesaving message of Jesus, or John on the rocky island of Patmos as he wrote Revelation. Both of these men were pillars of our faith who did some of their best work from jail. God blessed them immensely with the knowledge that others were coming to faith in Christ through Paul and John. Paul goes so far as to say, "I consider everything a loss because of the surpassing worth of knowing Christ Jesus my Lord" (Philippians 3:8, NIV).[10]

The Book of Matthew contains one of the most beautiful of all understandings of being blessed Matthew 5: 3- 11 (NRSV),

"Blessed are the poor in spirit, for theirs is the kingdom of heaven.
Blessed are those who mourn, for they will be comforted.
Blessed are the meek, for they will inherit the earth.
Blessed are those who hunger and thirst for righteousness, for they will be filled.
Blessed are the merciful, for they will receive mercy.

---

[10] Philippians 3:8, (NIV)

Blessed are the pure in heart, for they will see God.
Blessed are the peacemakers, for they will be called
children of God.
Blessed are those who are persecuted for righteousness'
sake, for theirs is the kingdom of heaven.
Blessed are you when people revile you and persecute you
and utter all kinds of evil against you falsely on my
account. Rejoice and be glad, for your reward is great in
heaven, for in the same way they persecuted the prophets
who were before you."[11]

The section of scripture known as "The Beatitudes" is the
beginning of Jesus' Sermon on the Mount ... one of a handful of
teachings that Jesus shared via the Gospels. Two Greek words are
used in the New Testament for "Blessed." They are Εὐλογητὸς
and μακάριος. The first means "a good word" or "to speak well"
while the second means "happiness or good fortune."[12] In The
Beatitudes, it is most often referring to the second type of blessing,
being happy in spite of misfortune within the life of the believer.

Blessed Are the Poor in Spirit

Billy Graham was asked what it meant to be poor in spirit.
Here is his response:

But Jesus also said that there is another kind of spiritual
poverty—one we should seek. He said, "Blessed are the
poor in spirit, for theirs is the kingdom of heaven"
(Matthew 5:3). What did He mean? Simply this: We must
be humble in our spirits. If you put the word "humble" in
place of the word "poor," you will understand what He
meant.

---

[11] Matthew 5:3-11, (NRSV)

[12] *Dictionary.com, s.v.* "Blessed," accessed January 25, 2017,
http://www.dictionary.com/browse/blessed

In other words, when we come to God, we must realize our own sin and our spiritual emptiness and poverty. We must not be self-satisfied or proud in our hearts, thinking we don't really need God. If we are, God cannot bless us. The Bible says, "God opposes the proud but gives grace to the humble" (James 4:6).

Pride can take all kinds of forms, but the worst is spiritual pride. Often the richer we are in things, the poorer we are in our hearts. Have you faced your own need of Christ? Do you realize that you are a sinner and need God's forgiveness? Don't let pride or anything else get in the way, but turn to Christ in humility and faith—and He will bless you and save you.[13]

Are you humble enough to ask Jesus to help you with THE TOTALITY OF YOUR LIFE? Are you willing to let him see those things that you keep hidden in the deepest recesses of your heart?

_____

_____

_____

How would the meaning of the Beatitudes change if you replaced the word "poor" with the word "humble" as Billy Graham suggests? (re-read Matthew 5:3 as you replace "poor" with the word "humble."

_____

_____

---

[13] Graham, Billy. *Answers.* BillyGraham.org. September 1, 2004. (https://billygraham.org/answer/what-does-it-mean-to-be-poor-in-spirit-as-jesus-said-we-ought-to-be / (accessed March 21, 2017).

Blessed Are They Who Mourn

> It is not enough for us ... within the arena of the world's pain merely to know of a God who sympathizes. It is not even enough to know of a God who heals. We need to know of and be connected with a God who experiences with us, for us, each grief, each wound. We need to be bonded with a God who has had nails in the hands and a spear in the heart![14]

How does it make you feel to know that God empathizes your inmost hurts and fears? (Empathy defined is, "the ability to understand and share the feelings of another.")[15]

_____

_____

_____

> Dietrich Bonhoeffer once said, "The disciples bear the suffering laid on them only by the power of him who bears all suffering on the Cross. As bearers of suffering, they stand in communion with the crucified. They stand as strangers in the power of him who was so alien to the world that it crucified him. This is their comfort, or rather, he is their comfort, their comforter. ... This alien community is comforted by the Cross."[16]

---

[14] Wuellner, Flora Slosson. *Weavings.* via *Blessed Are Those Who Mourn.* ChristianityToday.com. July 2004. http://www.christianitytoday.com/ct/2007/july/22.50.html (accessed March 21, 2017).

[15] Merriam Webster Dictionary. Empathy. Merriam-Webster.com. https://www.merriam-webster.com/dictionary/empathy (accessed March 21, 2017).

[16] Bonhoeffer, Dietrich. *Discipleship.* via *Blessed Are Those Who Mourn.* ChristianityToday.com. July 2004. http://www.christianitytoday.com/ct/2007/july/22.50.html (accessed March 21, 2017).

How does it make you feel to know that we can relate to Jesus as we share in His suffering here on this earth? We can empathize with Christ just as he empathizes with us. He comforts us and helps us to carry the load so that we do not break under the load's weight.

_____

_____

_____

How we bear our cross makes all the difference. Look at the stories of Peter (Luke 22: 54-62) and Judas (Matthew 27:3-5) and how they ended very differently. What is the difference in how they most likely mourned (which we may not know) and how they lived from that moment forward (which we do know)?

_____

_____

_____

Blessed Are The Meek

Matthew 5:5 (NIV)[17] says, "Blessed are the meek, for they will inherit the earth." Let's talk about the inheritance first. In Luke 15, the Prodigal Son salivates over his inheritance to the point where he receives it early. Romans 8:17 (NIV) very clearly states that if we believe in Jesus Christ as our Lord and Savior, then we become "Heirs of God and co-heirs with Jesus Christ."[18] Inheriting something good is always a beautiful thing. When we combine our inheritance from God with meekness, we increase our potential for good things exponentially. Take the Prodigal Son. I

---

[17] Matthew 5:5, (NIV)
[18] Romans 8:17, (NIV)

believe that his lack of meekness was his downfall. His dad allowed him to have the inheritance out of love. Once the son spent his inheritance, the Prodigal learned meekness via a grand dosage of humility. While he lost all of his money, he gained the world in realizing the preciousness of being in his Father's arms back home. The absence of meekness breeds pride and arrogance. The presence of meekness creates a far greater earthly and heavenly prize than we can imagine. The story of the Prodigal Son might have ended very differently. Instead of insisting upon his inheritance and wasting it away, he might have lived under his father's tutelage and received the inheritance and more after his father's death. Meekness combined with the younger son's inheritance would only have strengthened the younger son's long-term blessing.

Strong's concordance states that "*Biblical* meekness is *not weakness* but rather refers to exercising *God's strength* under *His control* – i.e. demonstrating power without undue harshness."[19] When I became an Ordained Elder, in the Service of Ordination my Bishop said to "take thou authority." It did not mean that I could use power as a tool of manipulation as the world does. Rather, it means that I promise to exercise the use of God's power only as He wills. Casting vision becomes a huge task as we carry out God's agenda. Casting vision is based on finding God's will rather than acting on my whims or desires.

As Strong's has said, the word "meek" does not mean that we are weak or a doormat for people to walk over. Rather, meekness means that by God's strength and under His control we can be confident and bold as we grow the Church. Too little confidence in God's ability to move mountains or too much confidence in our own power both have the same result, a lack of meekness. Meekness is about being the hands and feet of Jesus as we execute God's will in the world in which we live.

How do you handle power that is given to you?

---

[19] *Strong's Exhaustive Concordance: New American Standard Bible.* 1995. Updated ed. La Habra: Lockman Foundation. Accessed January 25, 2017. http://biblehub.com/greek/4239.htm.

_____

_____

What can happen if we abuse the power entrusted to us?

_____

_____

_____

How do we cast Godly vision in our workplaces, with our families, and within our churches?

_____

_____

_____

Blessed Are Those Who Hunger and Thirst for Righteousness

Matthew 5:6 (NIV) says, "Blessed are those who hunger and thirst for righteousness, for they shall be filled."[20] Taking a look at it from Eugene Peterson's *The Message*, he phrases it this way, "You're blessed when you've worked up a good appetite for God. He's food and drink in the best meal you'll ever eat" (Matthew 5:6, MSG).[21] How do we "work up a good appetite for God"? I recently participated in Dr. Elmer Town's *The Daniel Fast* during Lent. In 40 days I lost 30 pounds. As I fasted, I

_____

[20] Matthew 5:6 (NIV)
[21] Matthew 5:6 (The Message)

34

found myself more in tune with the Spirit of God.

During the first few days of my physical fast (not eating meat, not drinking anything but water, eating only plant-based foods), I was a mess. My body disengaged from the lifestyle that it knew. My energy was lacking. As I adapted to the fast with soy-based proteins, fruits, veggies, and nuts, I found myself having more energy than I did when eating everything that I wanted to eat (namely things like steak, fried foods, ice cream, etc.). My appetite for those other foods did not go away. I still loved them. But I no longer craved them, because I found a better way. I could go with my family to a Cracker Barrel and not crave the biscuits they were eating in front of me.

The message found in Matthew 5:6 is talking about this very phenomenon I found through the Daniel Fast. When we fall in love with God, we no longer crave the former things of the world. We still live in the world and work in the world. We do not want to engage in destructive behaviors that are not of God. We come to the place where we want to please God because God is worthy of our praise, and He blesses us in return as we seek him without end. Hunger and thirst can indicate one of two conditions. It can indicate "I WANT" or it can indicate "I NEED." We have a great many "WANTS." We have few actual "NEEDS." God is our greatest need.

From what habits do you need to fast (unhealthy or bad habits):

Spiritually?

_____

_____

_____

Physically?

_____

_____

_____

Emotionally?

_____

_____

_____

Let's talk about good habits in which to engage (good habits). What habits will you engage in to make you healthy:

Spiritually?

_____

_____

_____

Physically?

_____

_____

_____

Emotionally?

_____

_____

Blessed Are the Merciful

Matthew 5:7 (NIV) says, "Blessed are the merciful, for they will receive mercy."[22] Revisiting Peterson, his close paraphrase (taken from the original language) says, "You're blessed when you care. At the moment of being 'care-full,' you find yourselves cared for" (Matthew 5:7, MSG).[23]

In a study of 132 patients with multiple sclerosis (MS), researchers formed two groups, one of the people who met weekly to learn coping skills and another of people who met monthly and received support from another person with multiple sclerosis. The goal was to see which group fared better, those learning coping skills or those hearing from another MS sufferer.

The surprise finding was that neither group fared as well as did the five MS sufferers who had been trained to offer support. The study found that "giving support improved health more than receiving it." Those five MS sufferers felt a dramatic change in how they viewed themselves and life. Depression, self-confidence, and self-esteem improved markedly. The main researcher said, "These people had undergone a spiritual transformation that gave them a refreshed view of who they were." Caring for others brought healing for the caregivers.[24]

How can you be "care-full" this week?

---

[22] Matthew 5:7, (NIV)

[23] Matthew 5:7 (MSG)

[24] Moll, Rob, (2014) *What Your Body Knows About God* (Downers Grove, Illnois: InterVarsity Press), 108.

Matthew 5:7 is counter-intuitive. It requires that we give something away to receive the blessing of Almighty God in return. Mercy is so much more than showing grace when someone has wronged us. Mercy has a willingness to care for another person even when our flesh cries out in our own inner pain. The classic case of showing mercy in scripture comes from the story of the unforgiving servant. He owed more money to the king than he could ever repay. The king stood ready to forgive and forget until the king received word that the servant did not forgive. Caring and showing mercy not only does others right, but showing mercy heals us in the process. What a blessing!

To whom do you need to show mercy this week?

_____

_____

_____

Blessed Are the Pure in Heart

Matthew 5:8 (NIV) says, "Blessed are the pure in heart, for they will see God."[25] Eugene Peterson's *The Message* says, "You're blessed when you get your inside world—your mind and heart—put right. Then you can see God in the outside world" (Matthew 5:8, MSG).[26] We can control little in the world. We think that we are in control until the unimaginable happens. The external world around us is often spinning and we cannot stop it. We cannot stop time from moving forward just as we often cannot

---

[25] Matthew 5:8 (NIV)
[26] Matthew 5:8 (MSG)

stop the world from being unfair to us. But we can control how our inner soul relates to our outer world.

Proverbs 19:21 (NIV) says, "Many are the plans in a person's heart, but it is the Lord's purpose that prevails." How do we "let go and let God," especially when our hearts are slow to align with the will of God? (a friend of mine once said, "We have to act our way into a new way of thinking instead of thinking our way into a new way of acting.")

_____

_____

_____

I recently had a discussion with a young man about his job. I said, "It must be hard for you to have to hire and fire people on a daily basis. That would be so difficult for me." He responded by saying, "I have an internal switch. When I leave the office, I make sure that I flip the switch so that I do not take home with me a lot of the difficulties that I've faced during the day." I also remember recently telling a friend in conversation, "When I walk out of the door of my office at the end of the day, I make sure that I have a visual image in the back of my mind of leaving my keys on my desk as I walk out the door. It allows me to understand the great difference between my occupation and my familial lives. If I turn in my keys tomorrow, I can do so with the knowledge that I did not allow my family life to be devastated by spending too much time focused on my occupation."

What happens when our hearts are not in the right place before God?

_____

_____

Haggai 1:6 suggests five ways that we miss out when our hearts are not in the right place before God:

- we plant much, but we harvest little
- we eat, but we are never full
- we drink, but are never filled
- we put on clothes, but are not warm
- we earn wages, only to put them in a purse with holes in it

How do these words of Haggai apply to our lives?

_____

_____

_____

Blessed Are the Peacemakers

Matthew 5:9 (NIV) says, "Blessed are the peacemakers, for they will be called children of God."[27] *The Message* says, "You're blessed when you can show people how to cooperate instead of compete or fight. That's when you discover who you really are, and your place in God's family" (Matthew 5:9, MSG).[28] One of the hardest parts of being a minister is confrontation ... I strongly dislike it! If you were to truly get to know me, you would know at my core I like an approach of "Can't we all just get along!"

What is your core personality like and how would you benefit from being a peacemaker more often? Re-read Eugene Peterson's version of Matthew 5:9.

_____

[27] Matthew 5:9 (NIV)
[28] Matthew 5:9 (MSG)

_____

_____

_____

    Robert Goldman produced a fascinating study in the 1980's in which he asked Olympic athletes if they would cheat in order to win. They would take an undetectable drug with just one minor drawback ... within five years it would kill them. 52% of respondents said that they would take the drug.[29] OVER HALF! They decided that winning was much more important than the overall long-term affects to their health. When I think of the Barry Bonds, Mark McGwire, and the Alex Rodriguez's of the present day, I gain a much clearer picture of how being on top can lead people to "sell their souls to the devil" in order to win. Imagine how much greater Barry Bond's legacy in baseball would be if he did not dope. Hank Aaron would be more of a distant memory. Barry Bonds may be the all-time home run leader without the asterisks next to his name. The asterisk denotes that while he hit the most home runs, Hank Aaron's 715 home runs still stands as the all-time record.

    We could mention countless examples, but the point remains the same. The only true way to find long term success and blessing is in Jesus. We may not dope, but we have our own vices. We may focus on an unhealthy way to win in the business world or human relationships. We sacrifice the true joy we could experience if were to invite Jesus to define our agenda and then to join us on the journey enroute to success. Jesus did not win at all costs. He allowed himself to be beaten, killed, and go to hell (literally) just so that he could win the long-term goal of redemption and eternal life for us. Philippians 3:14 (NIV) gives the best recipe for personal winning, "I press on toward the goal to win the prize for which God has called me heavenward in Christ

---

[29] Goldman, Robert; Ronald Klatz (1992). _Death in the locker room: drugs & sports_ (2 ed.). Elite Sports Medicine Publications. 24.

Jesus."[30]

How competitive are you? Are you competitive in the right ways, building others up as you compete?

_____

_____

_____

     Notice in Peterson's version of Matthew 5:9, he uses the word "fight." The desire to fight can be a very negative and damaging emotion. While it might be helpful to "fight off an enemy" or to "fight for our lives," fighting as we know it leads to bitterness and adverse health effects. "When our bodies are constantly primed to fight someone, the increase in blood pressure and in chemicals such as C-reactive protein eventually take a toll on the heart and other parts of the body. The data that negative mental states cause heart problems is just stupendous," says Dr Charles Raison, clinical director of the Mind-Body Program at Emory University. "The data is just as established as smoking, and the size of the effect is the same."[31]
     Why would we want to purposefully harm our bodies? Ephesians 4:26 says, "In your anger do not sin: Do not let the sun go down while you are still angry." Maybe Paul knew in AD 60 something that we have medically proven in recent years. Anger, bitterness, and fighting not only can harm relationships … they also have the ability to harm us and our ability to be blessed. We are robbed of a healthy life on earth.

What fights do you need to resolve in order to find peace in your life? How might resolving a conflict lead to positive effects in your life?

_____

[30] Philippians 3:14 (NIV)

[31] Cohen, Elizabeth. "Blaming Others Can Ruin Your Health." CNN.com. http://www.cnn.com/2011/HEALTH/08/17/bitter.resentful.ep/ (accessed January 28, 2017).

_____

_____

_____

Matthew 5:10 (MSG) goes hand in hand with 5:11-12.
Eugene Peterson in *The Message* puts it this way:

> You're blessed when your commitment to God provokes
> persecution. The persecution drives you even deeper into
> God's kingdom. Not only that—count yourselves blessed
> every time people put you down or throw you out or speak
> lies about you to discredit me. What it means is that the
> truth is too close for comfort and they are uncomfortable.
> You can be glad when that happens—give a cheer,
> even!—for though they don't like it, I do! And all heaven
> applauds. And know that you are in good company. My
> prophets and witnesses have always gotten into this kind of
> trouble.[32]

How would God want us to respond to persecution? How might
you honor God by the way you react to conflict or persecution this
week?

_____

_____

_____

RECEIVE PRAYER REQUESTS BEFORE JOINING IN
UNISON IN THE CLOSING PRAYER:

Dear Lord, thank you for today. I rejoice in my relationship

_____

[32] Matthew 5:10-12 (MSG)

with you. I realize that I will encounter difficulties in this life, but that you have already won the victory. Help me to see the opportunities of each new day as I focus not on the problems I face, but on how you stand ready to bring a blessing in the midst of the storm. Thank you for loving me and for Jesus. In whose name I pray, AMEN.

HOMEWORK: READ SESSION THREE AND WRITE DOWN YOUR ANSWERS TO THE QUESTIONS FOR GROUP DISCUSSION BEFORE THE NEXT GROUP SESSION

www.TheBlessedLifeBook.com

SESSION THREE

Redefining Prosperity

OPEN THE BIBLE STUDY SESSION WITH PRAYER. ASK GOD TO BLESS YOUR TIME TOGETHER.

ANSWER THE QUESTIONS FOR GROUP DISCUSSION BELOW:

Prosperity is More Than Material Wealth

Billy Graham has built one of the most effective ministries in all the world, but he did so humbly.

> In 1950, his annual salary "was set at $15,000; at present, it is $39,500. In addition to his salary, of course, he receives full expenses while away from home, plus income from his writings. He has also inherited land valued at $420,000 and sold other inherited properties for $250,000. Although he has established trust funds for his children, much of the considerable income from his books has gone either to charitable causes or back into his ministry. He estimates, for example, that he gave away approximately $600,000 last year. He is thus financially comfortable but has not taken advantage of his position to build a personal fortune. His organization owns no airplane or stable of expensive automobiles; Graham's two personal cars are a Volvo and a Jeep."[33]

If you were given the physical resources that Billy Graham possessed during his ministry, what would you do to ensure that your treasure was found in God and not in material wealth? (see 1 Timothy 6:17-19 and Matthew 6:19-21)

---

[33] Martin, William. "The Power and Glory of Billy Graham." TexasMonthly.com http://www.texasmonthly.com/story/power-and-glory-billy-graham/page/0/7 (accessed January 28, 2017).

_____

_____

_____

 In John Wesley's sermon "The Use of Money," he gives a simple strategy in regards to how to manage economic prosperity. He boils it down to three simple rules for the use of money. Gain (or earn) all you can. Save all you can. Give all you can. When John Wesley began to teach the poor and lower class people of England about Biblical Wisdom as it relates to money, two unexpected but positive effects occurred. First, it spurred a revival that is credited with saving England from the violent revolutions that enveloped many of its other European counterparts. Second, the people he was preaching to learned how to be more responsible, better educated, and more prosperous. Wesley eventually faced a predicament where the Methodist were accumulating wealth, wearing better clothing, and building better homes and parsonages because they managed their money God's way.[34]
 Wesley would agree with the principle of "blessed to be a blessing." Blessed to be a blessing is the belief that if one is financially blessed, then he should be a blessing to someone else, especially if the other person is in need. Wesley felt that true compatibility of worldly wealth and Jesus can only be found as one uses his money in turn to spread the good news of Jesus Christ. Moreover, strict accountability must occur over the monies that are spent as a tool of protection and safeguard.

Are you currently tithing to the kingdom of God? The word tithe literally means "tenth." Maybe you have heard the 10/10/80 rule. Tithe 10%. Save 10%. Live on 80%. Sounds like a pretty good deal, doesn't it? Read Malachi 3:10, "Bring the whole tithe into the

_____

[34] Harnish, James, (2015) _Earn, Save, Give._ (Nashville: Abingdon Press), Kindle location 360 of 1442.

storehouse, that there may be food in my house. Test me in this," says the LORD Almighty, "and see if I will not throw open the floodgates of heaven and pour out so much blessing that there will not be room enough to store it."

_____

_____

_____

Are you currently in debt? If so, how can you develop a plan to get out of debt and live the life God intends for you to live?

_____

_____

_____

Check out Crown Financial Ministries at crown.org or Dave Ramsey's resources at DaveRamsey.com (including Financial Peace University). How can your church members grow in their understanding of God's plan for our money?

_____

_____

_____

Redefining Prosperity by Learning From Our Ancestors

Slavery in America from the 1600's to the 1870's is a remarkably dark chapter in American history. Though dark, the slaves found ways in which to nourish their inner faith in the midst of trying circumstances. The United Methodist Hymnal to this day still features several of the spirituals that were first sung by those in captivity.

The text of many spirituals, such as "Ezekiel Saw the Wheel" and "There Is a Balm in Gilead" came directly from the Old Testament. As he grieved over the sin of the Israelites who had turned their backs on God, the prophet Jeremiah posed the question, "Is there no balm in Gilead?" In their new religion, enslaved Africans found the answer in Jesus Christ.

There is a balm in Gilead to make the wounded whole;
There is a balm in Gilead, To heal the sin-sick soul.
Don't ever feel discouraged, for Jesus is your friend,
And if you lack for knowledge, he'll ne'er refuse to lend.[35]

These beautiful texts speak of a blessing that goes far beyond monetary wealth. Slaves were beaten and often imprisoned, and yet they found the ability to find an inner wealth in spite of their circumstances. Perhaps that is why Paul said in Philippians 1:21 (NIV), "... to live is Christ and to die is gain."[36] Paul knew oppression, including being shipwrecked and imprisoned.

If your material wealth were taken away tomorrow, how would you find happiness, joy, and peace?

_____

_____

_____

A favorite hymn of mine is Horatio Spafford's "It is Well

---

[35] Crosby, Pamela. "Part of History: African American Spirituals Still Heal." UMC.org http://www.umc.org/resources/part-of-history-african-american-spirituals-still-heal (accessed January 28, 2017).

[36] Philippians 1:21 (NIV)

With My Soul." In verse two, Spafford says, "Though Satan should buffet, though trials should come, Let this blest assurance control, That Christ hath regarded my helpless estate, And hath shed His own blood for my soul." In other words, real prosperity and blessing are found in Jesus alone. It is not a matter of the outer circumstances of life; rather, it is always a matter of the inner soul being in tune with God. A prominent Chicago businessman, Spafford had a beautiful wife, Anna, and four daughters (ages 11, 5, 9, and 2). Spafford was friends with Evangelist Dwight L Moody. In 1871, many of the properties that Spafford owned were destroyed by the Chicago fire, leaving him in financial ruin. Two years later, the Spaffords prepared to take a vacation, choosing England because Moody was going to preach there and the family wanted to hear him preach. Spafford sent his family ahead of himself because he had business to take care of before joining his family in England. "November 22, 1873, while crossing the Atlantic on the steamship *Ville du Havre*, their ship was struck by an iron sailing vessel, and 226 people lost their lives, including all four of Spafford's daughters. Anna Spafford survived the tragedy. Upon arriving in England, she sent a telegram to Spafford beginning "Saved alone." Spafford then sailed to England, passing near the location of his daughters' deaths. According to Bertha Spafford Vester, a daughter born after the tragedy, Spafford wrote "It Is Well with My Soul" on this journey."[37]

I pray you never have to go through what Horatio Spafford experienced. How do we define wealth when those things we cherish the most are taken away from us?

---

[37] Gazal, Andre. *Encyclopedia of Christianity in the United States.* 1st ed. 1 vol. Edited by George Thomas Kurian and Mark A Lamport. New York: Rowman and Littlefield, 2016, p.2171.

God wants us to see prosperity not in economic terms, but in terms of the inner soul. Spafford knew the loss of both financial wealth and his family. If all of our material assets were taken away tomorrow, we should still find solace in the world in which we live. The greatest blessing of all is our relationship with God in Christ Jesus; it brings the greatest prosperity of all.

RECEIVE PRAYER REQUESTS BEFORE JOINING IN UNISON IN THE CLOSING PRAYER:

Dear Lord, thank you for my life. Thank you loving me and sending Jesus to die on the cross for my sins. Show me how to be rich in you everyday. Help me to not allow the things of this world to come in between my relationship with you. In Jesus' name, AMEN.

HOMEWORK: READ SESSION FOUR AND WRITE DOWN YOUR ANSWERS TO THE QUESTIONS FOR GROUP DISCUSSION BEFORE THE NEXT GROUP SESSION

www.TheBlessedLifeBook.com

SESSION FOUR
How to Increase the Frequency of Blessing

OPEN THE BIBLE STUDY SESSION WITH PRAYER. ASK
GOD TO BLESS YOUR TIME TOGETHER.

ANSWER THE QUESTIONS FOR GROUP DISCUSSION
BELOW:

Several years ago, I remember watching a famous
televangelist preach on the subject of blessings. She said at one
time in her life she realized that she was missing out on the
blessings God had in store for her. She believed that the reason for
the missed blessing arose out of her lack of positivity and her lack
of being a blessing to someone else.

A simple truth emerges in the world in which we live: a
lack of feeling the blessings of God can come from many sources,
but the results are the same... WE DO NOT FEEL BLESSED!
We all want good things to happen to us. We want to succeed
mightily in everything that we do. But there are circumstances in
this world that we can control that sometimes choke off the flow of
blessings that come into our lives. Think about it like a water
hose. The difference between a wet water hose and a dry hose is
determined by the flow of water that comes through the water
faucet. If the water faucet is turned on, we can water our plants
and wash our cars. If the water faucet is turned off, the water will
remain in the pipe on the other side but will be of no benefit to us.
God wants us to turn the "water faucet" of our lives on full blast so
that potential blessings can turn into realized blessings.

Are you a negative or a positive person? Are you "the glass is half
empty" or "the glass is half full" kind of person? What can you do
to increase the frequency of blessing in your life this week?

Diminishing Potential Blessings

Let's talk in more detail about factors that diminish our potential blessings. These factors choke off the flow of blessings into our lives. Many of the factors fall within what we historically know as the "Seven Deadly Sins" as listed in Proverbs 6:16-19. The term "Seven Deadly Sins" was originally coined by a group of early Christians known as the Desert Fathers. They lived primarily in the geographical area of present-day Egypt.[38] John Cassian exported the term to Catholic circles in Europe where it was used to describe a host of sins that Christians needed to confess their sins for and avoid in the future. Cassian lived from 360-435 A.D. After Cassian wrote of The Seven Deadly Sins in his book *The Institutes*, the term became part of mainstream Christianity.[39]

Eugene Peterson's *The Message* does an excellent job of translating The Seven Deadly Sins found in Proverbs 6:16-19 into common terms.

Proverbs 6:16-19 (MSG)

Here are six things God hates,
    and one more that he loathes with a passion:
#1) eyes that are arrogant,
#2) a tongue that lies,
#3) hands that murder the innocent,
#4) a heart that hatches evil plots,
#5) feet that race down a wicked track,
#6) a mouth that lies under oath,

---

[38] Evagrius (2006). *Evagrius of Pontus: The Greek Ascetic Corpus translated by Robert E. Sinkewicz*. Oxford and New York: Oxford University Press.

[39] Cassian, John (2000). *The Institutes*. Newman Press of the Paulist Press.

#7) a troublemaker in the family.[40]

In Galatians 5: 19-21 (NIV), we find a parallel to The Seven Deadly Sins. Paul gives a larger list of temptations to avoid. In verse 21, Paul says that those who commit any of these sins "will not inherit the Kingdom of God."[41]

> Galatians 5: 19-21 (MSG): It is obvious what kind of life develops out of trying to get your own way all the time:
> 1) repetitive, loveless, cheap sex;
> 2) a stinking accumulation of mental and emotional garbage;
> 3) frenzied and joyless grabs for happiness;
> 4) trinket gods;
> 5) magic-show religion;
> 6) paranoid loneliness;
> 7) cutthroat competition;
> 8) all-consuming-yet-never-satisfied wants;
> 9) a brutal temper;
> 10) an impotence to love or be loved;
> 11) divided homes and divided lives;
> 12) small-minded and lopsided pursuits;
> 13) the vicious habit of depersonalizing everyone into a rival;
> 14) uncontrolled and uncontrollable addictions;
> 15) ugly parodies of community. I could go on.
>
> This isn't the first time I have warned you, you know. If you use your freedom this way, you will not inherit God's kingdom.[42]

In Galatians, Peterson writes Paul's words in the modern language as Paul says, "I could go on." While the list is a good list to put on our bathroom mirrors and avoid, it is only a partial list.

---

[40] Proverbs 6:16-19 (MSG)

[41] Galatians 5:21, (NIV)

[42] Galatians 5:19-21, (MSG)

Avoiding these sins helps to bring us blessing as we are centered in our relationship with God in Jesus Christ.

Which "sins" on this list do you find yourself struggling with the most? What can you do this week to ensure that you separate yourself from your struggles and find *The Blessed Life*?

_____

_____

_____

Increasing Potential Blessings

In A.D. 590, Pope Gregory I rewrote the categories of The Seven Deadly Sins as a more common list that we know in present day (and which Dante used in *The Divine Comedy*. They are *"pride, avarice, envy, wrath, lust, gluttony, and sloth/acedia."* The Catholic Church felt that people also needed virtues for which to strive, so they created "The Seven Holy Virtues." They are humility, generosity, kindness, patience, chastity, temperance, and diligence. Each of these virtues corresponds to one of the Seven Deadly Sins.[43]

Kindness vs. Envy
Humility vs. Pride
Diligence vs. Sloth
Generosity vs. Greed
Temperance vs. Gluttony
Chastity vs. Lust
Patience vs. Wrath

Let's take a closer look at each of the Holy Virtues in

---

[43] Hoopes, Tom and April. "7 Passion Sins and Virtues." NCRegister.com http://www.ncregister.com/site/article/7-passion-sins-and-virtues (accessed January 31, 2017).

greater detail, especially as we aspire to unlock the fountains of blessing in our lives. We may do well in several of these areas. We realize that with a few of the Holy Virtues, there will be room for improvement. It is okay! Mark 2:17 (NIV) says, "On hearing this, Jesus said to them, 'It is not the healthy who need a doctor, but the sick. I have not come to call the righteous, but sinners.'[44] We likely struggle with at least one or two. The goal here is not to be downtrodden or to say that we cannot do it. Rather, call upon the Holy Spirit to give us the power to do the impossible as learn how to embrace each of the Seven Holy Virtues.

Kindness

Kindness is a Holy Virtue and a Fruit of the Spirit (as mentioned in Galatians 5:22). Variations of the word kindness are mentioned in the Bible 78 times (kindness, lovingkindness, and loving kindnesses)[45] In the vein of mercy and grace, kindness refers to a close relationship with God. Kindness allows for redemption of human sin (Romans 2:4). God's kindness reconnects God to creation (Psalm 145:9) even when creation takes God's kindness for granted (Matt 5:45, Luke 6:35). Kindness comes into full view in our salvation offered through Jesus Christ (1 Peter 2:3).

Scripture tells us that it is more important to be kind to our fellow humanity than to offer ritual sacrifices to God (Hosea 6:6, Matthew 9:13, 12:7). God wants us to value kindness (Micah 6:8) and show kindness and mercy to others (Luke 6:35-36). Kindness is a Christian virtue (Colossians 3:12). Paul wanted to express kindness as a way to increase the authenticity of his ministry (2 Corinthians 6:6).[46]

When pitted against envy, we see how kindness relates to

---

[44] Mark 2:17, (NIV)

[45] "How Many Times is Kindness Mentioned in the Bible?" Answers.com http://www.answers.com/Q/How_many_times_is_the_word_%27kindness%27_used_in_th e_Bible (accessed July 31, 2017).

[46] Elwell, Walter A., ed. *Baker's Evangelical Dictionary of Biblical Theology.* (Grand Rapids: Baker Books, 1996) Accessed January 31, 2017. http://www.biblestudytools.com/dictionary/kindness/.

experiencing God's blessings in our lives. The kind Christian is concerned with glorifying God and making sure that he does not disappoint God. The kind Christian is full of God's grace and good will; he wants what is best for others. Others see a person of kind character and emulate the behavior back to the individual who initiated it. Kindness is a great blessing to receive from someone else. While not always sought after, kindness is always welcomed.

I think back on many of the relationships that I have built through the years. More often than not, the blessings that I have in my life are with me because of kind relationships. Others are returning the blessings to me that I've shown historically. I never formed the relationships to be blessed, but they seem to have a way of coming back around to me with a blessing. One friend, Pacer Joyner, helped me when I needed it with our new preschool in Waycross. I had a finite amount of money and a big job to move forward. Pacer never wavered in his willingness to say, "Yes, I'll help!" He did the job for about half of what others charged me. It was a blessing that allowed our preschool to open on time and near budget. In a sermon I watched of Joel Osteen one Sunday, he said that he remembered being kind to a person many years ago. When the time came for his church to overcome a significant hurdle they faced, the person he knew long ago was standing in the doorway of the decision. This person could either give the church what it desired or deny it. The person granted the church's request. The person said afterward that years ago Joel had shown them kindness. It was now time for this person to return the favor.

In contrast, the envious person wants what the other person has, be it a relationship or material possession. Envy is a dangerous emotion. It comes with a willingness to hurt others to get ahead. Envy can lead managers to keep more capable employees sequestered just for self-gain. Envy can lead jealousy to form between friends; it causes close friends to drift apart. Envy in its truest form is "jealousy over someone else's blessings or achievements."[47]

Do you remember Cain and Abel? Cain was envious of

[47]Elwell, Walter A., ed. *Baker's Evangelical Dictionary of Biblical Theology*. (Grand Rapids: Baker Books, 1996) Accessed January 31, 2017.
http://www.biblestudytools.com/dictionaries/bakers-evangelical-dictionary/envy.html.

Abel because Abel's offerings to God were accepted and Cain's were not. Granted, Cain did not give his best to God. Even so, it created a vicious envy within Cain that culminated in the death of Abel. Had Cain shown kindness to Abel every step of the way, the entire crisis could be averted. The seeds of destruction would not have grown. Who knows? Maybe the story might be about the blessing of forgiveness Cain received when he submitted his offering for the second time and took back his first fruits to God. We'll never know.

The Proverbs encourage us not to hang around envious (or jealous and unkind) people (Proverbs 24:1). As Nelson Searcy said long ago in a coaching session in Orlando, Florida, "We become the sum total of the five people we hang around the most." If we hang around envious people, we are more likely to become envious. If we are around kind people, we are more likely to be kind. Recently I met one of my son Maddux's teachers at the local elementary school. She radiated kindness. I asked others after my encounter with her if she was that way all of the time. They not only affirmed her kindness, but they also said she was even nicer than I could imagine. Such a Godly example of kindness impressed me. I gave God praise that my son could experience such a kind presence every day in school.

God has given us the gift of human choice, and God wants us to protect ourselves. God wants us to seek mentors and friends who are kind and can hold us accountable for being kind to others. Kindness leads to great blessing in our relationship with Jesus and other people.

Showing and receiving kindness is a two-step process. First, show kindness; then, receive the blessings of others and ultimately Almighty God as they are kind in return!

Give practical examples of kindness that you can show to others this week.

_____

_____

Name at least two people who need kindness shown to them. Commit yourself to being the ambassador of kindness to them. (It was be even better if these two people need to know the Lord, and your kindness to them is the first step in their journey to finding Jesus.)

Megan Jordan teaches that we should help our children to learn a series of questions in order to practice kindness. The questions allow children to evaluate how to be kind, especially during difficult circumstances. I find these questions to be useful not only with our children, but the questions would be useful for adults to ask as well:

Ask Themselves (of others):
1) How would that would make him feel?
2) How would that make me feel?
3) Look at her face: What do I think she's thinking right now?
4) Is she maybe feeling lonely or left out?
5) What else might he be upset about?

When Fighting, Ask:
1) Is it necessary to fight about this?
2) Is it worth being right or even just winning?
3) Did I [do something that hurt their feelings] just to be cool?

Ask Others:

1) Are you okay?
2) Is there anything I can do to help?
3) Is there anything you need?
4) Want to play?[48]

How can these questions be useful to us as we seek to be kind each day?

_____

_____

_____

Humility

One of the least attractive qualities of our human race is arrogance. Arrogance is the belief that someone is "that good." When he can deliver, often arrogance takes him to an even higher level of ability, because others look at the person and say, "He is great at what he does; he may flaunt it, but he knows what he is doing." The difficulty with arrogance is that when someone fails, he falls hard. Not only does he have to deal with the reality that he has failed, but he deals with a flawed self-perception of being too good to fail.

Think of examples of people in the world who you would define as "too good to fail." Who are they and how do they make you feel?

_____

_____

_____

[48] Joyner, Megan. *12 Questions That Teach Kindness In Your Children*. Babble.com https://www.babble.com/babble-voices/12-questions-that-teach-kindness-in-your-children/ (accessed March 22, 2017).

I believe that I can accomplish incredible things. I do so from the power and strength of the Holy Spirit. With God's help, I can move mountains and do the impossible (Matthew 19:26 and Mark 10:27). Without God's help, I will fail. In Judges 16, Sampson had the power of almighty God within him as he had never cut his hair before out of reverence for God. Delilah cut it, and Sampson lost his power. Sampson needed his hair locks which ultimately had their origins in God's providence. After his enemies had overtaken him, Sampson cried out to Almighty God and made the pillars of the temple fall, killing him and his enemies in the process. Sampson accomplished great tasks, but only by the power of God. We need to be humble enough to admit that we need help and yet confident enough to believe that we are up to a good challenge. Confidence requires humility. Without humility, confidence becomes arrogance.

How do you define humility? Who do you know who possesses true humility?

_____

_____

_____

How does it make you feel when you experience someone with true humility?

_____

_____

_____

Humility is the absence of self and the presence of Christ Jesus within our hearts. In Mark 8:35 (NIV), Jesus says, "For whoever wants to save their life will lose it, but whoever loses

60

their life for me and for the gospel will save it."[49] Worldly possessions and status may last for a time, but it is finite at best. Jesus was able to withstand Satan's attempts to get Jesus to sin in the desert during the 40-days fast because he knew the temptations were only for a short time. Satan could offer only temporal satisfaction. Only in a relationship with Jesus Christ grounded in self-denial and biblical confidence can we survive for all eternity. In Philippians 1:6 (NIV), Paul tells the church of Philippi, "being confident of this, that he who began a good work in you will carry it on to completion until the day of Christ Jesus."[50] Confidence rooted in humility is found in Christ alone.

Diligence

One of my favorite stories of Scripture comes from Genesis 32:22-31. I hope you will take the time to read it soon. Jacob crossed the ford of the Jabbok. When he was left alone, Jacob came into contact with a "man" whom Jacob believes in verse 30 to be God. Jacob wrestled with the man as the man tried passionately to break free. Jacob tells the man that Jacob would only let the man go if he blessed Jacob. In verse 29, the man blesses Jacob. Jacob was persistent in his pursuit of blessing, and he received a blessing in return.

Are you prepared to diligently wrestle with God until you experience His blessings?

_____

_____

_____

I am awed by some components of this Scripture. The man (God) changed Jacob's name to Israel. Israel means "he

_____

[49] Mark 8:34 (NIV)
[50] Philippians 1:6 (NIV)

struggles with God." Jacob struggled with God. The nation of Israel (God's chosen nation) struggled with God. God's people still struggle with God in the present day. To use a metaphor, I hear people frequently say, "Look to the light at the end of the tunnel." In railroad terms, a train in the tunnel experiences darkness. Even though it is moving forward, it will not experience daylight again until it is out of the tunnel. The challenge for the train is to keep moving forward until it reaches the light at the end of the tunnel.

You and I are like the train in the tunnel sometimes. We may feel momentary darkness, but it is important for us to keep moving forward in our faith. Even though we struggle and wrestle in our lives, God will bless us if we keep seeking Him as we move forward. Many times, God is the force that we need to go forward out of the darkness into the blessed life.

Recently, a mechanic friend of mine told me something interesting about our church bus. He said, "Barry, do you know what causes this bus to have problems?" I thought he was going to say running it too hard or misuse. He didn't. He said, "It has problems when it sits still too long." It also reminds me of the ages old phrase that says "an idle mind is the devil's workshop." The challenge for us is not to waste away physically, emotionally, or spiritually. Another wise person once said, "If you are not moving forward, you are moving backward." God has given us brilliant minds to use for His will and glory so that we can, in turn, be blessed. We need to be diligent to keep pressing forward into His perfect and pleasing will so that we can be blessed. Our heart's cry should be, "God, I'm pursuing you with everything I've got! Unlike Jacob, though, I will never let you go, God! Please bless me!" God will hear our cries for help and answer our prayers!

How can you be diligent as you keep moving forward through faith in Jesus Christ? Where do you need to be "unstuck"?

Generosity

Billy Graham is famous for generosity. While no official "Billy Graham Principle of Generosity" exists, nonetheless, a concept of generosity can be attributed to him. At many a workshop and speaking engagement, Graham has shared with participants to be generous in their tipping when they are out in the community. The reason that he says to give tips above and beyond the base requirement is two-fold.

First, generosity in tipping says something about the collective group's representation. Those waitresses, housekeepers, and others in the area know that a Christian group is having their workshop and are generous in spirit. When we tip generously (even though we do not have to!), it represents our witness of Jesus Christ. Cash on the pillow may be accompanied by simple note that says, "Thanks for what you do... God bless you. I'm praying for you." Our generosity may be the difference between someone coming to Christ or having a negative view of the Christian Church. I know that I would love to get up to Heaven and know that I did everything possible to win souls for Christ. If a few extra bucks or ten spot makes that difference, I am happy to be generous in order to win souls for Christ.

Second, the tip may bless the individual in ways that we cannot imagine. An extra dollar or two could mean the difference between someone being able to pay their electricity bill, feed their family, purchase a needed prescription, or obtain another heartfelt need. We never know what is going on in the life of someone else. He may look okay on the outside, but on the inside may be in the midst of real turmoil. God knows his situation and by the power of the Holy Spirit can meet his needs through us as we follow His lead.

2 Corinthians 9:6-8 (NIV) says, "Remember this: Whoever sows sparingly will also reap sparingly, and whoever sows

generously will also reap generously. Each of you should give what you have decided in your heart to give, not reluctantly or under compulsion, for God loves a cheerful giver. And God is able to bless you abundantly, so that in all things at all times, having all that you need, you will abound in every good work."

Generosity is about much more than our pocketbooks. How can you be generous this week?

_____

_____

_____

Temperance

At the heart of temperance is a willingness to find common ground with other people. In John 17: 20-23 (NRSV), Jesus is talking to God and praying on behalf of people that he loves dearly. He says,

> I do not ask for these only, but also for those who will believe in me through their word, that they may all be one, just as you, Father, are in me, and I in you, that they also may be in us, so that the world may believe that you have sent me. The glory that you have given me I have given to them, that they may be one even as we are one, I in them and you in me, that they may become perfectly one, so that the world may know that you sent me and loved them even as you loved me.[51]

Jesus prayed for all who would call upon His name to be one, and a watching world would be drawn to belief in Christ (John 17:20-21). He wanted the people to put their differences aside for the common belief that they would have in Him. Acts

---

[51] John 17:20-23 (NRSV)

1:12-14 (NRSV) emphasizes the unity they felt as they put aside their differences and focused on their relationship with Jesus Christ. The disciples and others gathered in the upper room plainly disagreed on many things. But, they realized that they could be unified and of "one accord" as they believed in Jesus as their Lord and Savior.

> Then they returned to Jerusalem from the mount called Olivet, which is near Jerusalem, a Sabbath day's journey away. And when they had entered, they went up to the upper room, where they were staying, Peter and John and James and Andrew, Philip and Thomas, Bartholomew and Matthew, James the son of Alphaeus and Simon the Zealot and Judas the son of James. All these with one accord were devoting themselves to prayer, together with the women and Mary the mother of Jesus, and his brothers. [52]

As C.S. Lewis said, temperance means "going to the right length and no further."[53] Even though we are different and disagree on so much, we find unity in Jesus Christ.

How might our churches change if we practiced temperance in Jesus Christ more?

_____

        .
_____

_____

How might our world change if we practice temperance in Jesus Christ more?

_____

[52] Acts 1:12-14 (NRSV)
[53] Lewis, *Mere Christianity*, 78-79.

Chastity

Bishop Michael Watson once stood before the South Georgia Annual Conference and emphasized the importance of being celibate in singleness and honoring matrimony in marriage. In other words, we commit ourselves to making sure that we do not have sex outside of marriage. Within marriage, we commit to being faithful to one spouse for as long as we both shall live.

Putting this understanding up against the word "lust," we gain a very clear understanding of God's desire for us as it relates to sex. God created Adam and Eve to enjoy each other and to fill the earth with offspring. As we live in a fallen world, we often see how sex, a beautiful gift from God, had been corrupted to embrace meanings that are absent of what God intends. We see the continual destruction of marriages and relationships when one spouse chooses to have a relationship with someone who is not his or her spouse.

Adam Hamilton, a United Methodist minister, recently wrote about a staff situation where two ministers, one female and one male, chose to engage in an adulterous affair. The situation included a number of victims. The church suffered. The family of those who were involved in the affair suffered. And the two who engaged in the affair lost their ministerial statuses for life. They had to find new jobs outside of ministry. And for what? All because they allowed lust to consume their lives.

The United Methodist Church is not immune to the larger world. In a recent situation involving the leaked identities of Ashley Madison users (an adultery website), many ministers throughout Methodism were disciplined and / or defrocked because of their inappropriate engagement with the website and / or other users on the website.

Chastity is about purity. It is about being people of

Christian character when dating and living within the bounds of marriage in a God-honoring way. We must put up boundaries that will keep us above contempt, because God and others are watching. Sex is a true blessing from God. It is fantastic! But it is only good when used in the appropriate way. God wants us to value celibacy in singleness and matrimony in marriage. Whether Christian or not, that is good advice to follow. In Christian circles, chastity is sure to increase our ability to find blessing.

How do we honor celibacy in singleness and matrimony in marriage in a way that is God honoring? (see Revelation 2:3-5)

_____

_____

_____

Patience

　　Have you ever prayed for God to give you patience? God may test us with certain situations because trials develop patience. 1 Corinthians 10:13 (NIV) provides us great news when we pray for patience, "No temptation has overtaken you except what is common to mankind. And God is faithful; he will not let you be tempted beyond what you can bear. But when you are tempted, he will also provide a way out so that you can endure it."[54] Patience is a learned attribute and not something that we naturally possess. Patience is something that we must cultivate as we choose how to respond to situations that we encounter. As a wise person once shared with me, "You cannot make me angry; I can choose to be mad at you." Patience recognizes that we may not control our initial emotion of anger, but we can control our reaction. As we pray for God's strength, He will give you the ability to stand up to almost any obstacle.

---

[54] 1 Corinthians 10:13, (NIV)

Proverbs 14:29 (NIV): "Whoever is patient has great understanding, but one who is quick-tempered displays folly.[55]

Romans 12:12 (NIV): "Be joyful in hope, patient in affliction, faithful in prayer."[56]

Proverbs 16:32 (NIV): "Better a patient person than a warrior, one with self-control than one who takes a city."[57]

How do we practice becoming a more patient person of God?

_____

_____

_____

What value do we find when we are patient in the kingdom of God?

_____

_____

_____

RECEIVE PRAYER REQUESTS BEFORE JOINING IN UNISON IN THE CLOSING PRAYER:

Dear Lord, thank you for the blessings you bring into my life on a daily basis. Help me to increase the blessings of God and decrease anything that comes in the way of you blessing me. I pray for those areas of struggle for which I am most vulnerable. May your hedge of protection be over me so that I

---

[55] Proverbs 14:29, (NIV)

[56] Romans 12:12, (NIV)

[57] Proverbs 16:32, (NIV)

may avoid sin, worship you through my lifestyle choices, and give you the glory for every good and perfect gift that comes into my life. In Jesus' name, AMEN.

HOMEWORK: READ SESSION FIVE AND WRITE DOWN YOUR ANSWERS TO THE QUESTIONS FOR GROUP DISCUSSION BEFORE THE NEXT GROUP SESSION

www.TheBlessedLifeBook.com

SECTION TWO

Historical Giants who Lived the Blessed Life and
What They Have to Say about Blessings

SESSION FIVE

A Study of John Wesley, His Failures, and Successes

OPEN THE BIBLE STUDY SESSION WITH PRAYER. ASK GOD TO BLESS YOUR TIME TOGETHER.

ANSWER THE QUESTIONS FOR GROUP DISCUSSION BELOW:

Nowhere is the concept of blessing more alive than in the life and ministry of John Wesley. Wesley knew what it meant to be both a failure and a resounding success.

Saved From The Fire

When he was five years old, a fire destroyed his family home. On February 9, 1709, around 11 p.m., all of the children of Samuel Wesley's house made it safely out of the house except for John who was stuck on a second-floor balcony. Just before the roof collapsed, volunteers were able to reach John by standing on each other's shoulders. Wesley later coined the statement, "a brand plucked out of the fire,"[58] quoting Zechariah 3:2 (NIV).[59] Life itself was a blessing for Wesley because of what he experienced. Being saved from the fire at the age of five was a chance for him to enjoy everyday life yet again as he received a heart of gratitude for being saved from the fire.

When have you or someone you love experienced a moment when you were "a brand plucked out of the fire"? What was the moment and did you realize that God's hand was at work in your life at that moment?

---

[58] Wallace, Charles Jr, (1997) *Susanna Wesley : the complete writings*, (New York : Oxford University Press), 67.
[59] Zechariah 3:2, (NIV)

America: Successful Pastorate; Unsuccessful Experience with Love

When John Wesley first came to the American colonies, he landed at Fort Pulaski and made his way to the new English settlement known as Savannah, Georgia which was established by General James Oglethorpe. Wesley took over for the Rev. Quincy, who was still in Savannah. Wesley would arrive February 5, 1736, but not occupy his parsonage until Rev. Quincy's departure in March. During the cold winter month of February, Wesley spent his nights aboard *The Simmonds*, the same ship on which he and others sailed into port.

During his time in Georgia, Wesley experienced the joys of somewhat successful ministry as well as the agony of returning to England as a scorned man. On Sundays his workday was full. He preached, followed by participating in a worship experience with the Moravians. From 5 a.m. - 6:30 a.m., he read prayers in English. At 9 a.m., he would read prayers in Italian to a small group of people known as the Vaudios. From 10:30 a.m.-12:30 p.m., he held an English service with a full sermon and Holy Communion. At 1 p.m., he held a French service. At 2 p.m., he taught a group of children. At 3 p.m., he held evening prayer vespers. After the 3 p.m. vespers, he gathered a large group together for prayer, scripture reading, and praise. At 6 p.m., he finished his day as an attendee at the Moravian worship service. At one point during his time in America, he wrote in his journal how it seemed that his life and ministry were going well.

His life gradually began to turn for the worse as Wesley became involved with Sophia Hopkey. For a short time, Sophia was at Fort Frederica with Charles Wesley. As background, James Oglethorpe had great plans for John Wesley to be one of General

Oglethorpe's trusted leaders when John first arrived. James Oglethorpe decided it would be good to set up his new single preacher (John) with an available woman in the area (Sophia). After her experience at Frederica, Sophia wanted to return to England. She could not stand to be in the colonies any longer.

John Wesley, perhaps from good intentions gone wrong, encouraged Sophia to stay in Georgia. He pleaded with her until she finally agreed and had a change of heart. When John saw General Oglethorpe again, the General took no notice of John. Sophia comforted John and said, "Sir, you encouraged me in my greatest trials; be not discouraged yourself. Fear nothing; if Mr. Oglethorpe will not, God will help you."[60]

Sophia began to view John in a romantic light. She asked General Oglethorpe what the "appropriate dress" would be when she shared company with John. She wore only white dresses to honor John. In December 1736, he writes that he lost "not only 'all the colour of my remaining life' for her, but perhaps all my happiness too, in time and in eternity."[61] By February 1737, with the help of Charles Delamotte and the Moravians, Wesley determined not to marry Sophia. In March 1737, Sophia quickly married a Mr. Williamson. Wesley said that Williamson was "not remarkable for handsomeness, neither for greatness, neither for wit, or knowledge, or sense, and least of all for religion." Wesley made the following entry in his journal: "On Saturday, March 12th, God being very merciful to me, my friend performed what I could not."[62]

July 3, 1737, Wesley shared with Sophia points in her behavior that needed improvement. In August 1737, Wesley refused to offer her communion. Mr. Thomas Causton, uncle of Sophia, a local storekeeper, and chief magistrate of the area, quickly drew up ten counts of grievances against Wesley within the civilian court system. Wesley was summoned to appear before the grand jury. Mr. Causton fixed the jury and trial to ensure a

---

[60] Telford, John (1994) *The Life of John Wesley*. (Nicholasville, KY: Schmul Publishing Company), book found online at http://wesley.nnu.edu/?id=88, accessed November 20, 2015.

[61] Telford, *The Life of John Wesley*.

[62] Telford, *The Life of John Wesley*.

conviction of John Wesley. On Friday, December 2, 1737, after evening prayers, Wesley boarded a boat bound for the Carolinas and eventually for England. The relationship with Sophia had become his downfall.

What relationships or life events should we insulate and protect ourselves from because they have the potential to be our downfall if left unattended?

_____

_____

_____

      Here's the truth: Not everyone hated John Wesley in America. Many loved him. John Wesley found success in his ministry in the Americas. WOW! George Whitefield speaks of Wesley's ministry in the Americas by saying, "What the good Mr. John Wesley has done in America is inexpressible. His name is very precious among the people, and he has laid a foundation that I hope neither men nor devils will ever be able to shake. Oh that I may follow him as he has followed Christ."[63]

Looking back on a failure in your life, what are the life lessons you may have learned?

_____

_____

_____

      John was left to feel like a failure when he left Savannah because of the resistance that he encountered. His heart was hurt. For so many of us, the raging reality of our lives is that we go

---

[63] Telford, *The Life of John Wesley.*

along doing very well until resistance comes our way. For many of us when confronted with the need to either "fight or take flight," we take flight too soon. Imagine how Wesley's story would be different in the Americas if he had allowed Sophia to go back to England (when she initially wanted to leave) or offered her Holy Communion. After all, the people to whom I serve Holy Communion are sinners in need of divine grace anyway! Sure, John Wesley faced a no-win situation as those who controlled the civilian court system could throw him in jail. And yet when George Whitefield looked back on Wesley's ministry and his conduct in America, Whitefield saw the success of Wesley's ministry. Wesley was a failure in his own eyes even though he was beloved by many.

How can others help us to evaluate our failures?

_____

_____

_____

It is unmistakable that God used Wesley in Georgia and his ministry was blessed. How we can learn from this situation! God wants us to realize that many of the "failures" of our lives may be a blessing for someone else. Sometimes God wants us to redefine our definition of success. We are sinful, yes. Are we broken? Absolutely. But God can use us, sinful and broken as we are, to build His kingdom through us as he blesses others with the life-saving message of Jesus Christ.

Have you ever experienced a failure that brought an unexpected good or benefit into your life? Would you have noticed this opportunity if you had not failed?

_____

The Return to England: Heartache and Rebirth at Aldersgate

When John returned to England, his heart ached. He felt like a failure in his ministry and personal life. John wrote, "I, who went to America to convert others, was never myself converted to God."[64] The experience in the Americas had been tough on both Charles (John's brother) and John. They both were left to question their faith and their salvation.

Have you ever questioned your faith and salvation? How did God meet you in the moment to reaffirm His love for you?

Charles Wesley was the first to have a salvation experience. May 21, 1738, Charles wrote in his journal that the Holy Spirit "chased away [his] unbelief."[65] The author of some six to seven thousand hymns later wrote "And Can It Be That I Should Gain" as a tribute to his recommitment to Christ.

John Wesley was heavily influenced by a group of German Christians known as the Moravians. They were very mystic in their faith. Many believe that the mystery that Methodists still experience as it relates to Holy Communion and other church traditions still refers back to the influence that the Moravians had on John during his ministry. May 24, 1738, John was invited to go to a Moravian worship service on Aldersgate Street in London. He

[64] Telford, *The Life of John Wesley*.

[65] Green, Roger J. "1738 John and Charles Wesley Conversions." ChristianityToday.com http://www.christianitytoday.com/ch/1990/issue28/2844.html (accessed January 30, 2017).

wrote in his journal,

> In the evening I went very unwillingly to a society in Aldersgate Street, where one was reading Luther's preface to the Epistle to the Romans. About a quarter before nine, while he was describing the change which God works in the heart through faith in Christ, I felt my heart strangely warmed. I felt I did trust in Christ, Christ alone, for salvation; and an assurance was given me that He had taken away my sins, even mine, and saved me from the law of sin and death.

> I began to pray with all my might for those who had in a more especial manner despitefully used me and persecuted me. I then testified openly to all there what I now first felt in my heart. But it was not long before the enemy suggested, "This cannot be faith; for where is thy joy?" Then was I taught that peace and victory over sin are essential to faith in the Captain of our salvation; but that, as to the transports of joy that usually attend the beginning of it, especially in those who have mourned deeply, God sometimes giveth, sometimes withholdeth, them according to the counsels of His own will.

> After my return home, I was much buffeted with temptations, but I cried out, and they fled away. They returned again and again. I as often lifted up my eyes, and He "sent me help from his holy place." And herein I found the difference between this and my former state chiefly consisted. I was striving, yea, fighting with all my might under the law, as well as under grace. But then I was sometimes, if not often, conquered; now, I was always conqueror.

> Thursday, 25.—The moment I awakened, "Jesus, Master," was in my heart and in my mouth; and I found all my strength lay in keeping my eye fixed upon Him and my soul waiting on Him continually. Being again at St. Paul's in the afternoon, I could taste the good word of God in the anthem which began, "My song shall be always of the

loving-kindness of the Lord: with my mouth will I ever be showing forth thy truth from one generation to another." Yet the enemy injected a fear, "If thou dost believe, why is there not a more sensible change? I answered (yet not I), "That I know not. But, this I know, I have 'now peace with God.' And I sin not today, and Jesus my Master has forbidden me to take thought for the morrow."

Wednesday, June 7.—I determined, if God should permit, to retire for a short time into Germany. I had fully proposed, before I left Georgia, so to do if it should please God to bring me back to Europe. And I now clearly saw the time was come. My weak mind could not bear to be thus sawn asunder. And I hoped the conversing with those holy men who were themselves living witnesses of the full power of faith, and yet able to bear with those that are weak, would be a means, under God, of so establishing my soul that I might go on from faith to faith, and from "strength to strength."[66]

John would spend the next three months with the Moravians in Germany. His ministry was reshaped by what happened at Aldersgate. It is important to understand that Wesley knew all about high church and indeed had attended an evening worship service that same night at St. Paul's Cathedral of the Church of England. It would be similar to formal worship in the present. Ministers wear robes. Liturgy is valued. A formal order of worship includes hymns. But it was with a small group of Moravians that God changed John's life forever.

What came out of that night was a John Wesley who had a new self-assurance that God could help him surmount the foibles that had dogged him most of his life. The smaller community of accountability and reflection gave Wesley something he had benefited from many years earlier in

[66] "The Journal of John Wesley: I Felt My Heart Strangely Warmed," Christian Classics Ethereal Library. accessed January 30, 2017, https://www.ccel.org/ccel/wesley/journal.vi.ii.xvi.html.

Oxford. Here was a group that knew him, that knew his struggles, and who helped him overcome his questions of faith. They gave him time to reflect and then commune with the heavenly Father who sought to reestablish a relationship with John.[67]

Many through the years have ventured various thoughts as to why Aldersgate was such a powerful experience for Wesley. My belief is that part of what Wesley experienced that night was an authentic giving of his life completely and wholly to God. Moreover, I believe that it was the first time he found true healing from the events that he experienced in Georgia. When our souls ache, it makes it hard for us to move forward on any front. Blessing comes as we finally allow the Holy Spirit to heal us in ways we cannot heal ourselves. We become complete and whole as we open our hearts to God. Then we move forward with a sense that there is no mountain that we cannot overcome.

Are you in need of healing? God wants to meet you right now to heal your hurts and redeem your perceived failures. Right them down. Let go and let God. He wants to carry your load.

_____

_____

_____

RECEIVE PRAYER REQUESTS BEFORE JOINING IN UNISON IN THE CLOSING PRAYER:

Dear Lord, thank you for your great love for me. Thank you that you love me-- failures and all. Be with me as I seek to learn from my failures and find the positive within the difficult

_____

[67] Whitesel, Bob, "A Holistic Good News: Missional, Effective Evangelism And Lessons Learned While Traveling in the Hoof Prints of Wesley." The Great Commission Research Journal. Vol. 5, No. 1, Summer 2013.

circumstances of my life. **Heal my hurts and calm my fears as I trust in you daily. In Jesus' name, AMEN.**

HOMEWORK: READ SESSION SIX AND WRITE DOWN YOUR ANSWERS TO THE QUESTIONS FOR GROUP DISCUSSION BEFORE THE NEXT GROUP SESSION

www.TheBlessedLifeBook.com

SESSION SIX

The Blessings of Billy Graham

BEFORE THE BIBLE STUDY: CHECK OUT
BillyGraham.org and BillyGrahamLibrary.org

OPEN THE BIBLE STUDY SESSION WITH PRAYER. ASK
GOD TO BLESS YOUR TIME TOGETHER.

ANSWER THE QUESTIONS FOR GROUP DISCUSSION
BELOW:

     Few men in the world have had as great an impact as Billy
Graham. In the 1950's, Billy was in the heyday of his ministry in
America with a somewhat fiery persona that inspired packed
stadiums to commit to Jesus Christ. He traveled to the former
USSR and South Africa at a time when Communism and
Apartheid were in full force. He has completed over 400 crusades
in over 185 countries on six continents. He held a crusade in
London that lasted for twelve weeks[68] and one in New York City's
Madison Square Garden that lasted for sixteen.[69] In a word, his
ministry and world impact are astounding. Let's look at a few of
the factors that made Billy the real deal not only as a minister but
as an incredibly blessed man who has blessed countless others.
What are the secrets to Graham's blessed life? Let's look at
several factors in more detail.

His Wife: Ruth Graham

     It is true that behind every good man is a good woman.
Surprisingly, behind Billy Graham, was a well educated lifelong
Presbyterian who refused to undergo baptism by immersion. Ruth

---

[68] "Crusade City Spotlight: London." BillyGrahamLibrary.org
http://billygrahamlibrary.org/crusade-city-spotlight-london/ (accessed February 1, 2017).
[69] "1957 New York Crusade." BillyGrahamLibrary.org
http://billygrahamlibrary.org/1957-new-york-crusade/ (accessed February 1, 2017).

Graham and Billy were married in 1943 at Montreat Presbyterian Church, a church that Ruth would continue to attend and call home until her death in 2007.[70]

What is most remarkable about Billy and Ruth Graham is that all five children followed their parents into the ministry. Out of 19 grandchildren, three have become Christian preachers.[71] Ruth's legacy is not only that of a devoted wife who blessed her husband. She realized the importance of passing on her faith to her children, grandchildren, and great-grandchildren.

At the age of 13, Ruth was sent by her parents into Pyeng Yang Foreign School in what is now Pyongyang, North Korea. She felt very homesick and read all 150 Psalms to help her cope. Later, she would say that those moments in Korea were her "boot camp" that helped her faith not only to have a firm foundation, but also to find peace in the midst of being separated from those that she loved the most.

Ruth's parents, Dr. Nelson and Virginia Bell, were medical missionaries at Love and Mercy Hospital in Tsingkiangpu, China, from 1916 until 1941. Ruth grew up in an environment of political turmoil as she experienced the 1911 Chinese revolution and the Japanese invasion of China and fall of Shanghai (the capital of China at the time) in 1937. With the fall of Shanghai, she would be evacuated from China in a troop carrier ship and go on to Wheaton College where she and Billy would meet and later fall in love.[72] Before meeting Billy, Ruth thought about being a missionary in Tibet and never marrying. After Billy, she could only imagine her life with one man--namely Billy Graham.

Ruth used her voice in her marriage with Billy. Ruth was raised in a family of women who would speak their minds, often before the men would ask for the lady's opinion. Billy was raised

[70] "Billy Graham: She Was a Wonderful Woman." ChristianityToday.com http://www.christiantoday.com/article/billy.graham.she.was.a.wonderful.woman/11168.htm (accessed February 1, 2017).

[71] Miller, Lisa. "The Fight Over Billy Graham's Legacy." NewsWeek.com http://www.newsweek.com/fight-over-billy-grahams-legacy-67527 (accessed February 1, 2017).

[72] Driscolli, Kristen. "Ruth Bell Graham: A Life Well Lived." BillyGraham.org http://billygraham.org/decision-magazine/june-2013/ruth-bell-graham-a-life-well-lived/ (accessed February 1, 2017).

in a family where the male was the head and women were quiet. Billy quickly learned the value of listening to Ruth's opinion!

Anne Graham Lotz, the Grahams' second daughter, said, "My daddy didn't have to seek my mother's advice to get it. I remember a time she [told] about him fussing at her because he just didn't want her opinion. He does not like opinionated women, and he [had] a house full of them. It takes awhile for a man who's been living independently to take on his partner and consult her. I think in some of those stories Daddy was just learning to be a husband. ... Today he would not only consult her opinion, he would respect it and honor it and listen to her."[73]

At Ruth's funeral in 2007, Billy in unscheduled remarks stood up on the front row and said of Ruth, "Ruth was an incredible woman. I wish you could look in her casket because she is so beautiful. I sat there a long time last night looking at her, and I prayed, because I knew she had a great reception in heaven.[74]

Ruth and Billy were blessed in their marriage. August 13, 2003, they celebrated their 60th wedding anniversary. Ruth said of the momentous occasion, "There was some adjusting during the first few years, but it has pretty well adjusted now." Billy remarked, "We have a better relationship now. We look into each other's eyes and touch each other. It gets better as you get older. The secret is the Lord Jesus Christ–to have Him in the center of our lives."[75]

Their marriage is a testimony to a Godly marriage. Theirs was a marriage of infinite blessing. It may not have been perfect, but it was one from which the fountain of blessings flowed as they had their foundation in Jesus Christ.

---

[73] Driscolli, "Ruth Graham".

[74] Olsen, Ted. "Ruth Graham's Public Funeral." ChristianityToday.com http://www.christianitytoday.com/gleanings/2007/june/ruth-grahams-public-funeral.html (accessed February 1, 2017).

[75] Driscolli, Kristen. "Ruth Graham: A Life Well Lived, Part 2." http://billygraham.org/decision-magazine/june-2013/ruth-bell-graham-a-life-well-lived-part-2/ (accessed February 1, 2017).

How might Billy's impact have been different had Ruth not been a part of his life? Imagine what it must have been like for Ruth when Billy called from Los Angeles and said, "Instead of a three week crusade, we are going to keep going for eight weeks. Is that okay?"

_____

_____

_____

Could Billy still accomplish his amazing feats in present day America? Why or why not?

_____

_____

_____

Graham's Children: Gigi, Anne, Ruth, Franklin, Nelson

Proverbs 22:6 (BBE)[76] "If a child is trained up in the right way, even when he is old he will not be turned away from it."

The Graham family is a testimony to generational blessings. From the beginning of the Christian scripture, we find that families can either be blessed or cursed by the values embodied by patriarch and the matriarch of the family. The Grahams are no different. Billy and Ruth taught their children the value of Christianity as a lifestyle. When their children became older, they could not imagine any other way than living for the Lord.

_____

[76] Proverbs 22:6, (BBE)

Paxton, my middle son who is five, has started to say to me, "Dad, when I grow up, I want to be a preacher just like you!" It scares me to death. What scares me is not that he intends to be a preacher. His decision honors me. What scares me is that my son is watching every move I make, both good and bad. He learns how to live his life from me. While he will certainly go through the growing pains of life, my decisions now will influence the life that he lives later. It is a big responsibility!

When God was giving the Ten Commandments to the people, He said in Exodus 20:5 (NIV), "You shall not bow down to [idols] or worship them; for I, the LORD your God, am a jealous God, punishing the children for the sin of the parents to the third and fourth generation of those who hate me..."[77] Wow! The actions the Hebrews took had consequences down to the third and fourth generation of those who came after them. It makes me even more terrified.

As you consider the concept of generational blessings, will you be like Billy and Ruth Graham and raise your children in the ways of the Lord? (see Proverbs 4:10-27)

_____

_____

_____

How can you begin now to teach your children about the Lord so that when they are older, they will not stray from God's commands (and if they do, it won't be for a lack of effort!)? (see Proverbs 22:6)

_____

_____

---

[77] Exodus 20:5 (NIV)

Billy and Ruth Graham are a source of blessing not only to their children but will continue to be a source of blessing for many generations to come. From the youngest of ages, our children depend on us for their life. Billy and Ruth made sure that their children were reared in the Lord and had the best possible childhoods imaginable. Now their children are a testament to the values and character that their parents instilled in them at an early age. The children of Billy Graham continually bless him because of the work that he and Ruth put into rearing their children at a young age.

What blessings may return to you because you raised your children in the Lord?

Civil Rights and Equality

Dr. Martin Luther King once said of Billy Graham, "Had it not been for the ministry of my good friend Dr. Billy Graham, my work in the Civil Rights Movement would not have been as successful as it has been."[78]

In 1957, Graham's stance towards integration became more publicly shown when he allowed African American ministers Thomas Kilgore and Gardner Taylor to serve as members of his New York Crusade's executive

---

[78] Freeze, Trevor. "Remembering Dr. Martin Luther King Jr." BillyGraham.org http://billygraham.org/story/remembering-dr-martin-luther-king-jr/ (accessed February 1, 2017).

committee[79] and invited the Rev. Martin Luther King, Jr., whom he first met during the Montgomery Bus Boycott in 1955,[80] to join him in the pulpit at his 16-week revival in New York City, where 2.3 million gathered at Madison Square Garden, Yankee Stadium, and Times Square to hear them.[81] Graham recalled in his autobiography that during this time, he and King developed a close friendship and that he was eventually one of the few people who referred to King as "Mike," a nickname which King asked only his closest friends to call him.[82] Following King's assassination in 1968, Graham mourned that America had lost "a social leader and a prophet."[83] In private, Graham would also advise King and other members of the Southern Christian Leadership Conference(SCLC).[84]

By the middle of 1960, King and Graham traveled together to the Tenth Baptist World Congress of the Baptist World Alliance.[85] In 1963, Graham posted bail for King to be released from jail during the civil rights protests in Birmingham.[86] Graham held integrated crusades in Birmingham, Alabama, on Easter 1964 in the aftermath of the bombing of the Sixteenth Street Baptist Church, and toured Alabama again in the wake of the violence that accompanied the first Selma to Montgomery march in 1965.[87]

Graham's faith prompted his maturing view of race and segregation; he told a member of the KKK that

[79] "William Franklin Graham." Standford.edu
http://kingencyclopedia.stanford.edu/encyclopedia/encyclopedia/enc_graham_william_frank
lin_1918/ (accessed February 1, 2017).

[80] "William Franklin Graham." Standford.edu

[81] Horstman, Barry. "Billy Graham: A Man with a Mission." Cincinatti Post
https://www.highbeam.com/doc/1G1-87912863.html (accessed February 1, 2017).

[82] Freeze, Trevor. "Remembering Dr. Martin Luther King Jr."

[83] "William Franklin Graham." Stanford.edu

[84] Miller, Steven P. (2009). *Billy Graham and the Rise of the Republican South*.
(Philadelphia: University of Pennsylvania Press) p. 92.

[85] "William Franklin Graham." Standford.edu

[86] Long, Michael, ed. *The Legacy of Billy Graham: Critical Reflections on America's Greatest Evangelist*, (Westminster: John Knox Press, 2008), 150–151.

[87] "William Franklin Graham." Standford.edu

integration was necessary primarily for religious reasons: "there is no scriptural basis for segregation," Graham argued, "The ground at the foot of the cross is level, and it touches my heart when I see whites standing shoulder to shoulder with blacks at the cross."[88][89]

I believe that the focus on Graham's involvement is important on several levels, but none is more important than the issue of God's blessings in the life of Billy Graham. He was able to leverage his national presence to assist in the cause of Civil Rights. He took a significant risk, yes. But his shared belief in God with his constituency allowed him to champion civil rights in ways many others could not achieve. Billy Graham was living through the same days as Harper Lee's *To Kill a Mockingbird*. He was a preacher of Southern heritage. God gave him a platform to use in a beautiful and mighty way. He chose to be obedient to God's will, even though he encountered resistance. God's blessing in the movement of civil rights was being able to be a voice for equality. Blessing in this circumstance was not about a feel-good experience. Graham's blessing was receiving God's power and authority to go and boldly proclaim the message of God.

I am reminded of the Prayer of Jabez as it speaks of how God wants to enlarge our territory. Bruce Wilkinson wrote a book of the same name. 1 Chronicles 4:10 (NIV) says, "Oh, that you would bless me and enlarge my territory! Let your hand be with me, and keep me from harm so that I will be free from pain. And God granted his request." Billy followed God and God enlarged his territory. God gave him a huge platform to use for the Kingdom, and Billy used it to further the cause of racial equality.

Read Matthew 25:35-40. How does Billy's fight for racial equality reconcile with this Scripture?

_____

---

[88] Horstman, "Billy Graham: A Man With a Mission". (accessed February 1, 2017).

[89] "Billy Graham." Wikipedia.org https://en.wikipedia.org/wiki/Billy_Graham (accessed February 1, 2017).

Appropriate Boundaries

"Billy Graham famously said he would not meet, eat, or travel with a woman alone. Not only was he protecting himself from temptation, but he was also protecting his marriage and ministry from any potentially damaging allegations."[90] I remember a story from my childhood in which Billy would not go into a motel room without it first being checked by his staff. His life was blessed because he had safeguards in place that kept him above reproach. Historically, kings dug moats around their palaces because they knew that it would be much harder for the enemy to get in. Presently, we need to build moats of protection around our lives so that we can preserve our blessings.

As I look at my life in the ministry over the 20 years that I've now been a United Methodist minister, I see that a lack of boundaries and safeguards can either make or break what we are trying to do for the Lord. Blessings that took a lifetime to build can be washed away in an instant. Thank God for examples like Billy Graham who go above and beyond to make sure that he kept his life above reproach. He was blessed in large measure because he had good safeguards in place.

As you think about the boundaries in your life, where do you need to strengthen your defenses so that the enemy does not invade your weaknesses to destroy your impact for the kingdom of God? (see Mark 9:50 and Ephesians 5:1-4)

---

[90] Gatliff, Cort. "Three Wise Safeguards in the Wake of Ashley Madison." TheGospelCoalition.org https://www.thegospelcoalition.org/article/3-wise-safeguards-in-the-wake-of-ashley-madiso n (accessed February 1, 2017).

A Life Rooted in Simplicity

      I recently read a blog post of Dr. Marc Baldwin. He was discussing simplicity, specifically as it related to Billy's delivery of the gospel message. Here's what Baldwin said.

> Billy Graham focused on a simple gospel message in his evangelistic sermons and crusades. Every sermon had a clear presentation of the Christian gospel, founded upon the message of John 3:16: "For God so loved the world that He sent His one and only Son that whoever believes in Him would not perish but have eternal life." That message was the heart and soul of every evangelistic crusade, everywhere he went. There was no need to reinvent himself every so often. Sometimes the best writing avoids contrivances, complex language, and complicated research. Certainly not all writing can be simplified for a popular audience but don't think that complex subjects always require complex presentation.[91]

      What impresses me most about Billy Graham is when he would do an altar call, he would do so with his text written out as to what he was going to say. Most ministers write their sermons out and then "wing it" when it comes to the altar call. Graham believed that the altar call was one of the most important elements of the service and therefore should be scripted to ensure that he gave it the proper attention that it deserved and so that it would be as successful as possible. Think about altar calls that you've seen Billy Graham perform. During the call, he always had "Just As I Am" played while he told people to come forward and respond to

---

[91]Baldwin, Marc. "Keeping It Simple: Billy Graham's Life Sermons Inspire Purity and Simplicity in Religious Writings." DrMarcBaldwin.com http://drmarcdbaldwin.com/2011/09/keeping-it-simple-billy-grahams-life-sermons-inspire-purity-and-simplicity-in-religious-writings/ (accessed February 1, 2017).

God's love. As they came forward, he always said something similar to "the buses will wait." If you watched many crusades, you noticed that the message did not change. It was simple. It was powerful. It provoked a profound response. Graham was always well-prepared to deliver the message. Millions came to know Jesus as a result of Graham's crusades.

Could there be a greater blessing in all the world than knowing that someone came to know Jesus as their personal Lord and Savior? Graham's life calling was to share Jesus, and he blessed the lives of countless others as they came to know Jesus.

God uses those who are ready. It is interesting that if the Billy Graham Crusade had 500 people to pray with the lost at the altar, they would have 450-600 decisions for Jesus. If the crusade had 2000 people ready to pray, they might save 1900-2100 souls. This pattern presented itself throughout Billy's ministry. Readiness to share the Gospel was always a prerequisite for souls saved. Are you PREPARED to bring others to Jesus Christ if the opportunity allows? Have you PRACTICED sharing the message in private so that you will be able to share publically when the time arrives? (Consider rhetorically as well: How many people have you brought to the Lord in your lifetime?)

_____

_____

_____

RECEIVE PRAYER REQUESTS BEFORE JOINING IN UNISON IN THE CLOSING PRAYER:

Dear Lord, thank you for your servant Billy Graham. Thank you that he was selfless and humble in his desire to see your Kingdom grow. His life was immensely blessed. Show me how to be the Billy Graham of my day, trusting in you as the source of never ending blessings in my life and receiving the

confidence to share Jesus with others each day. In Jesus' name, AMEN.

HOMEWORK: READ SESSION SEVEN AND WRITE DOWN YOUR ANSWERS TO THE QUESTIONS FOR GROUP DISCUSSION BEFORE THE NEXT GROUP SESSION

www.TheBlessedLifeBook.com

SESSION SEVEN

The Early Church Fathers and
Their Understandings of Blessings

OPEN THE BIBLE STUDY SESSION WITH PRAYER. ASK
GOD TO BLESS YOUR TIME TOGETHER.

ANSWER THE QUESTIONS FOR GROUP DISCUSSION
BELOW:

I am enamored with those who write about the Christian
faith. They often write with an eloquence and depth that I believe
is often missing in our present day world. I love the Early Church
Fathers. They are the people who built the foundation of
Christianity that we enjoy today. Without many of these early
Christians, we would not benefit from the vibrancy of belief and
faith in Christianity that we enjoy in the present day. Chew on
their words. Ask yourself, "What are my Christian ancestors
trying to say to me about blessings? How do the principles apply
to me in the present day?" Let's look at several of the Early
Church Fathers and flesh out brief passages of their writings as
they relate to blessings.

Gregory of Nyssa lived from 335-395 A.D. He was Bishop of
Nyssa. He, his older brother Basil of Caesarea, and their friend
Gregory of Nazianzus are collectively known as the Cappadocian
Fathers. He said the following in regards to blessings:

> It will not be unfitting to adapt the word of the prophet to
> our present blessings: "In the multitude of the sorrows
> which I had in my heart, the comforts of God," by your
> kindness, "have refreshed my soul," like sunbeams,
> cheering and warming our life nipped by frost. For both
> reached the highest pitch -- the severity of my troubles, I
> mean, on the one side, and the sweetness of your favours

93

on the other. And if you have so gladdened us, by only sending us the joyful tidings of your coming, that everything changed for us from extremest woe to a bright condition, what will your precious and benign coming, even the sight of it, do?[92]

Blessings come into our lives at the strangest times. Many times we find blessings in the midst of a sorrowful situation. He quotes Psalm 94:19 when he mentions "the word of the profit."

Consider the conundrum. Blessings and sorrow are often intertwined in our lives. Jesus saved us (A HUGE BLESSING!) at the same time that he was crucified (a time a sorrow). How do we notice the blessings of God in the midst of the sorrow of our lives? (see John 16:16-24)

_____

_____

_____

How can blessings help us to come through the sorrow that we experience in our lives? (see Psalm 30:5)

_____

_____

_____

Saint Augustine lived from 354-430 A. D. He was Bishop of Hippo Regius (modern-day Annaba, Algeria, Africa). Augustine gives two categories of blessings -- temporal (meaning in the here and now but not forever) and eternal (lasting forever). He then

---

[92] Gregory of Nyssa. "Letter VII: To A Friend." BibleStudyTools.com http://www.biblestudytools.com/history/early-church-fathers/post-nicene/vol-5-gregory-of-nyssa/gregory-of-nyssa/letter-vii-to-a-friend.html (accessed February 1, 2017).

defines which blessings fit into what category. Ultimately, Saint Augustine rightfully shares that God is the one who bestows all blessings. He said the following:

> There are then two kinds of blessings, temporal and eternal. Temporal blessings are health, substance, honour, friends, a home, children, a wife, and the other things of this life in which we are sojourners. We are put up then in the hostelry of this life as travellers passing on, and not as owners intending to remain. But eternal blessings are, first, eternal life itself, the incorruption and immortality of body and soul, the society of Angels, the heavenly city, glory unfailing, Father and father-land, the former without death, the latter without a foe. These blessings let us desire with all eagerness, let us ask with all perseverance, not with length of words, but with the witness of groans. Longing desire prayeth always, though the tongue be silent. If thou art ever longing, thou art ever praying. When sleepeth prayer? When desire groweth cold. So then let us beg for these eternal blessings with all eager desire, let us seek for those good things with an entire earnestness, let us ask for those good things with all assurance. For those good things do profit him that hath them, they cannot harm him. But those other temporal good things sometimes profit, and sometimes harm. Poverty hath profited many, and wealth hath harmed many; a private life hath profited many, and exalted honour hath harmed many. And again, money hath profited some, honourable distinction hath profited some; profited them who use them well; but from those who use them ill, the not withdrawing them hath harmed them more. And so, Brethren, let us ask for those temporal blessings too, but in moderation, being sure that if we do receive them, He giveth them, who knoweth what is expedient for us.[93]

---
[93] St. Augustine. "Sermon XXX." BibleStudyTools.com http://www.biblestudytools.com/history/early-church-fathers/nicene/vol-6-saint-augustin/select-sermons-gospels/sermon-xxx-lxxx-ben.html (accessed February 1, 2017).

Consider these two categories, temporal and eternal blessings. What are they in your life?

Temporal:

_____

_____

_____

Eternal:

_____

_____

_____

Are there any temporal blessings in your life you need to let go of in order to take hold of God's eternal blessings in your life? (see Ecclesiastes 1)

_____

_____

_____

Augustine discusses the blessed life in terms of our eternal relationship with God in Christ Jesus. He discusses the difficulties found in this life, especially found in relationships with others who do not have our best interests in mind. But, never fear! Augustine assures us that wicked and evil people will ultimately receive their due from God in his coming judgment.

O sensible man! If the wine in thy bottle is diminished,

thou art sad; days art thou losing, and art thou glad? These days then are evil; and so much the more evil, in that they are loved. This world is so alluring, that no one is willing to finish a life of sorrow. For the true, the blessed life is this, when we shall rise again, and reign with Christ. For the ungodly too shall rise again but to go into the fire. Life then is there again, but that which is blessed. And blessed life there can be none but that which is eternal, where are "good days"; and those not many days, but one day.[94]

Read Psalm 34:17-22. In what areas of your life do you currently feel downtrodden?

_____

_____

_____

How will God deliver you from the trials and tribulations that you currently face?

_____

_____

_____

Saint John Chrysostom lived from 349-407 A.D. He was Bishop of Constantinople. Chrysostom wanted those who believe in Jesus Christ to give thanks for the blessings bestowed upon others, because thankfulness allows us to rid ourselves of envy and be more generous and genuine in our human relationships.

But let us be thankful not for our own blessings alone, but

---

[94] St. Augustine. "Sermon XXX."

also for those of others; for in this way we shall be able both to destroy our envy, and to rivet our charity, and make it more genuine. Since it will not even be possible for thee to go on envying them, on behalf of whom thou givest thanks to the Lord.[95]

How has God blessed you? (see James 1:17)

_____

_____

_____

How can you be continually thankful for the blessings of God in your life? (see 1 Thessalonians 5:16-18)

_____

_____

_____

Have you ever considered a gratitude journal? (see Psalm 136)

Consider keeping a gratitude journal. Lauren Jessen writes:

Gratitude works its magic by serving as an antidote to negative emotions. It's like white blood cells for the soul, protecting us from cynicism, entitlement, anger, and resignation.

The best time to start a gratitude journal is now. These are the incredible benefits associated with journaling, and

[95] Saint John Chrysostom. "Homily XXV." BibleStudyTools.com http://www.biblestudytools.com/history/early-church-fathers/nicene/vol-10-saint-john-chryso stom/homilies-on-matthew/homily-xxv.html (accessed February 1, 2017).

because maintaining a journal can be challenging, I share the tips that work best for me:

Benefits of a Gratitude Journal
1. Lower stress levels.
2. Feel calm at night.
3. Gain a new perspective of what is important to you and what you truly appreciate in your life.
4. By noting what you are grateful for, you will gain clarity on what you want to have more of in your life, and what you can cut from you life.
5. Helps you focus on what really matters.
6. Keeping a gratitude journal helps you learn more about yourself and become more self-aware.
7. Your gratitude journal is a safe zone for your eyes only, so you can write anything you feel without judgment.
8. On days when you feel blue, read back through your gratitude journal to readjust your attitude and remember that you have great people and things in your life.

Maintaining a Gratitude Journal

1. Plan to write in your gratitude journal every night for 15 minutes before bed. Set an alarm reminder on your phone or schedule it in your calendar. I've found that it is easier to write at night so that I can include things that I am grateful for from that day.
2. Keep your gratitude journal by your nightstand so you will see it before going to sleep and remember to jot down what you are thankful for. Your journal may even become a symbol of gratitude so that when you just look at it, you will feel a sense of appreciation.
3. Write as many things as you want in your gratitude journal. Writing down 5-10 things that you are grateful for each day is a good number to aim for.
4. Your gratitude journal doesn't have to be deep. What you are thankful for can be as simple as "family" or "the

new book or movie I recently enjoyed" or "this morning's breakfast." What you are grateful for will differ from everyone else.
5. The timing of when you want to write is up to you.

While I try to write in my gratitude journal every night, sometimes it becomes every other night. That's okay. Journal when it feels right for you — the benefits really are worth it.[96]

John Chrysostom continues:

> Let us too therefore continually give thanks, for our own blessings, and for those of others, alike for the small and for the great. For though the gift be small, it is made great by being God's gift, or rather, there is nothing small that cometh from Him, not only because it is bestowed by Him, but also in its very nature.[97]

Blessings should first root be rooted in God's love. Love empowers blessings in our lives and allows us to experience a depth of blessings not otherwise possible. I am reminded of 1 John 4:8 (NIV), "Whoever does not love does not know God, because God is love."[98]

> For he who loveth rejoices not so much in commanding, as in being commanded, although to command is sweet: but love changes the nature of things and presents herself with all blessings in her hands, gentler than any mother, wealthier than any queen, and makes difficulties light and easy, causing out virtues to be facile, but vice very bitter to

---

[96] Jessen, Laura. The Benefits of a Gratitude Journal and How to Maintain One. HuffingtonPost.com http://www.huffingtonpost.com/lauren-jessen/gratitude-journal_b_7745854.html (accessed March 25, 2017).

[97] Saint John Chrysostom. "Homily XXV."

[98] 1 John 4:8, (NIV)

us.[99]

List the blessings of God that come to mind as a direct result of His great love for you.

_____

_____

_____

Tertullian lived from 155-240. He was an early Christian author from Carthage in the Roman province of Africa. Tertullian wrote that blessings are two-fold. First, God gives us the blessings that we enjoy. Second, we cannot experience the genuine depth of earthly blessings without first experiencing the full depth of God's blessings (i.e.- heavenly blessings).

> So are we first invited to heavenly blessings when we are separated from the world, and afterwards we thus find ourselves in the way of obtaining also earthly blessings. And your own gospel likewise has it in this wise: "Seek ye first the kingdom of God, and these things shall be added unto you."[100]

Tertullian says "we first [are] invited to heavenly blessings when we [are] separated from the world." How do you define heavenly blessings?

_____

_____

---

[99] Saint John Chrysostom. "Homily XXII." BibleStudyTools.com
http://www.biblestudytools.com/history/early-church-fathers/nicene/vol-12-saint-john-chrysostom/homilies-on-first-corinthians/homily-xxxii.html (accessed February 1, 2017).
[100] Tertullian. "Book III." BibleStudyTools.com
http://www.biblestudytools.com/history/early-church-fathers/ante-nicene/vol-3-latin-christianity/tertullian/book-iii.html (accessed February 1, 2017).

Tertullian says that heavenly blessings give rise to our ability to receive earthly blessings. In the context of Matthew 6:33, how does this influence your view of how we receive earthly blessings?

Clement of Rome died in the year 99 AD. He was known as Pope Clement I and St. Clement of Rome. Clement of Rome gives us a call to beware of false teachers -- namely, teachers of Christ who are false prophets. They give out false blessings. His remarks lead us to an understanding that teachers and preachers of the Word of God are called to a higher standard. As James 3:1 (NIV) reminds us, "Not many of you should become teachers, my fellow believers, because you know that we who teach will be judged more strictly."

> For because of the unruliness of the tongue cometh anger; but the perfect man keeps watch over his tongue, and loves his soul's life." For these are they "who by good words and fair speeches lead astray the hearts of the simple, and, while offering them blessings, lead them astray." Let us, therefore, fear the judgment which awaits teachers. For a severe judgment will those teachers receive "who teach, but do not," and those who take upon them the name of Christ falsely, and say: We teach the truth, and yet go wandering about idly, and exalt themselves, and make their boast" in the mind of the flesh."[101]

[101] Clement of Rome. "The First Epistle of Clement." BibleStudyTools.com http://www.biblestudytools.com/history/early-church-fathers/ante-nicene/vol-8-third-fourth-centuries/clement-of-rome/first-epistle-blessed-clement.html (accessed February 1, 2017).

Read 1 Timothy 4:1-5. A big part of *The Blessed Life* happens as we discern the right way to go and what to avoid in life. Based on this Scripture and others, what might fall into the category of false teachings?

_____

_____

_____

How can you test to see if somoeone is genuine in their teachings?

_____

_____

_____

How can you personally avoid being a false teacher?

_____

_____

_____

Ambrose lived from 340-397. He was also known as "Saint Ambrose," Bishop of Milan. Ambrose begins by telling us that virtue is the highest good and the fruit of a blessed life. Virtue includes attaining eternal life by faith in God. I love how he puts it! "A blessed life is the fruit of the present, and eternal life is the hope of the future!"[102] The blessed life to Ambrose is always

---

[102] Ambrose. "Book II." BibleStudyTools.com
http://www.biblestudytools.com/history/early-church-fathers/post-nicene/vol-10-ambrose/ambrose/book-ii.html (accessed February 1, 2017).

linked to the eternal implications of a relationship with the Lord. He realized that many could and have suffered through history, including those in the Bible such as Isaac, Jacob, Joseph, and Job. And yet, they were blessed as their faith gave them strength in many very harrowing experiences. Our faith can do the same for us in the present day.

It is quite certain that virtue is the only and the highest good; that it alone richly abounds in the fruit of a blessed life; that a blessed life, by means of which eternal life is won, does not depend on external or corporal benefits, but on virtue only. A blessed life is the fruit of the present, and eternal life is the hope of the future.

Some, however, there are who think a blessed life is impossible in this body, weak and fragile as it is. For in it one must suffer pain and grief, one must weep, one must be ill. So I could also say that a blessed life rests on bodily rejoicing, but not on the heights of wisdom, on the sweetness of conscience, or on the loftiness of virtue. It is not a blessed thing to be in the midst of suffering; but it is blessed to be victorious over it, and not to be cowed by the power of temporal pain.

Suppose that things come which are accounted terrible as regards the grief they cause, such as blindness, exile, hunger, violation of a daughter, loss of children. Who will deny that Isaac was blessed, who did not see in his old age, and yet gave blessings with his benediction? Was not Jacob blessed who, leaving his father's house, endured exile as a shepherd for pay, and mourned for the violated chastity of his daughter, and suffered hunger? Were they not blessed on whose good faith God received witness, as it is written: "The God of Abraham, the God of Isaac, and the God of Jacob"? A wretched thing is slavery, but Joseph was not wretched; nay, clearly he was blessed, when he whilst in slavery checked the lusts of his mistress. What shall I say of holy David who bewailed the death of three sons, and, what was even worse than this, his daughter's incestuous connection? How could he be unblessed from whom the Author of blessedness Himself sprung, Who has made many blessed? For: "Blessed are they who have not seen yet have believed." All these felt their own weakness, but they bravely prevailed over it. What can we think of as more wretched than holy Job, either in the burning of his house, or the instantaneous death of his ten sons, or his bodily pains? Was he less blessed than if he had not endured those things whereby he really showed himself approved?[103]

What is Christian virtue? (see Philippians 4:8)

_____

_____

_____

As you hear Ambrose discuss Christian virtue, consider what it means to "live for the Lord." If living for the Lord daily is the highest Christian virtue, how do you follow the example of the giants of Scripture mentioned by Ambrose to ensure that you follow God daily in spite of the persecutions you may face? (see Matthew 5:10)

_____

_____

_____

Discuss the role of sanctification in attaining Christian virtue. Sanctification is the process by which we continue to grow in

---
[103] Ambrose. "Book II."

holiness. A sanctuary is literally "a holy place." How do we grow in Christian sanctification and how does this relate to Christian virtue? (see Philippians 3:12-14)

_____

_____

_____

Ambrose discusses the blessed life in terms of outward show versus inward fortitude. Outward show brings with it the assurance of only temporal blessing. He relates blessing to Matthew 6 which says that things done in secret are far superior to outward show. Things done in secret come with eternal blessing.

> Blessed, plainly, is that life which is not valued at the estimation of outsiders, but is known, as judge of itself, by its own inner feelings. It needs no popular opinion as its reward in any way; nor has it any fear of punishments. Thus the less it strives for glory, the more it rises above it. For to those who seek for glory, that reward in the shape of present things is but a shadow of future ones, and is a hindrance to eternal life, as it is written in the Scriptures: "Verily, I say unto you, they have received their reward." This is said of those who, as it were, with the sound of a trumpet desire to make known to all the world the liberality they exercise towards the poor. It is the same, too, in the case of fasting, which is done but for outward show. "They have," he says, "their reward."

> It therefore belongs to a virtuous life to show mercy and to fast in secret; that thou mayest seem to be seeking a reward from thy God alone, and not from men. For he who seeks it from man has his reward, but he who seeks it from God has eternal life, which none can give but the Lord of Eternity, as it is said: "Verily, I say unto thee, today shalt thou be

with Me in Paradise." Wherefore the Scripture plainly has called that life which is blessed, eternal life. It has not been left to be appraised according to man's ideas on the subject, but has been entrusted to the divine judgment.[104]

Why does God care so much that we are humble rather than boastful? What happens when we are outwardly boastful but inwardly lacking in our relationship with God?

_____

_____

_____

Ambrose tells us that the blessed life is the reward of our good works rooted in our faith. The blessed life often rises out of some of the painful and hard experiences that we find in our life. Ambrose relates the New Testament Scriptures of Matthew 5:11 and Matthew 16:24.

> Innocence, then, and knowledge make a man blessed. We have also noted already that the blessedness of eternal life is the reward for good works. It remains, then, to show that when the patronage of pleasure or the fear of pain is despised (and the first of these one abhors as poor and effeminate, and the other as unmanly and weak), that then a blessed life can rise up in the midst of pain. This can easily be shown when we read: "Blessed are ye when men shall revile you and persecute you and shall say all manner of evil against you for righteousness' sake. Rejoice and be exceeding glad, for great is your reward in heaven; for so persecuted they the prophets which were before you." And again: "He that will come after Me, let him take up his cross and follow Me."[105]

---

[104] Ambrose. "Book II."
[105] Ambroise. "Book II."

What is the difference between good works rooted in faith versus good works just for the sake of good works?

_____

_____

_____

Origen lived from 184-253 A. D. He was a Christian theologian who spent the first half of his career in Alexandria. Origen was very particular that blessings are of a "spiritual nature." As I read the words of Origen, I am reminded of how good and evil exist in the world and constantly battle against each other. Blessings come as we trust in God, not only as good comes, but as God's hedge of protection over us to shield us from the evil that is in the world.

> Now, the injunctions to "depart from evil, and to do good," do not refer either to corporeal evils or corporeal blessings, as they are termed by some, nor to external things at all, but to blessings and evils of a spiritual kind; since he who departs from such evils, and performs such virtuous actions, will, as one who desires the true life, come to the enjoyment of it; and as one loving to see "good days," in which the word of righteousness will be the Sun, he will see them, God taking him away from this "present evil world," and from those evil days concerning which Paul said: "Redeeming the time, because the days are evil."[106]

Read 1 John 1:5. As you hear Origen's words, how do you respond to the battle between good and evil that exists in the world?

---

[106] Origen. "Book VI." BibleStudyTools.com
http://www.biblestudytools.com/history/early-church-fathers/ante-nicene/vol-4-third-century/ origen/book-vi.html (accessed February 1, 2017).

_____

_____

_____

RECEIVE PRAYER REQUESTS BEFORE JOINING IN
UNISON IN THE CLOSING PRAYER:

**Dear Lord, thank you for the Spiritual Giants who continue to
light the way in how to be blessed each day. May their legacy
teach me not only how to live out** *The Blessed Life* **but to be a
blessing to those around me. In Jesus' name, AMEN.**

HOMEWORK: READ SESSION EIGHT AND WRITE DOWN
YOUR ANSWERS TO THE QUESTIONS FOR GROUP
DISCUSSION BEFORE THE NEXT GROUP SESSION

www.TheBlessedLifeBook.com

SESSION EIGHT

More Recent Saints on the Role of Blessings in Our Lives

OPEN THE BIBLE STUDY SESSION WITH PRAYER. ASK GOD TO BLESS YOUR TIME TOGETHER.

ANSWER THE QUESTIONS FOR GROUP DISCUSSION BELOW

Oswald Chambers (1874-1917) was an evangelist and Bible teacher. His best-known work, *My Utmost for His Highest,* was a compilation of lectures, manuscripts, and notes comprised by his beloved wife after his death. In speaking of blessings, he talked about "the fountain of blessing" that comes when we have an equal flow of receiving the blessings of Almighty God and bestowing those blessings upon the hearts and lives of others. A deficit of either (receiving blessings from God or showering blessings upon others) will lead to an imbalance in the Christian life that leads to "dryness" or "deadness." Like a flowing river, blessings start with God in Christ Jesus, flow through us, and flow into the hearts and lives of others.

> We are to be fountains through which Jesus can flow as "rivers of living water" in blessing to everyone. Yet some of us are like the Dead Sea, always receiving but never giving, because our relationship is not right with the Lord Jesus. As surely as we receive blessings from Him, He will pour out blessings through us. But whenever the blessings are not being poured out in the same measure they are received, there is a defect in our relationship with Him. Is there anything between you and Jesus Christ? Is there anything hindering your faith in Him? If not, then Jesus says that out of you "will flow rivers of living water." It is not a blessing that you pass on, or an experience that you

share with others, but a river that continually flows through you. Stay at the Source, closely guarding your faith in Jesus Christ and your relationship to Him, and there will be a steady flow into the lives of others with no dryness or deadness whatsoever.[107]

Discuss the balance between receiving blessings from God and showing blessings to others. Why do you believe Oswald felt that an imbalance of between receiving God's blessings and showering them upon others could be a problem? (Think about the river of living water that is supposed to pour through us into the hearts and lives of others. See also John 7:38)

_____

_____

_____

Chambers shared that blessings are an outward expression of God's goodness to us. We must be careful to worship God himself, and not the blessings that God bestows. I am reminded of how we sometimes worship the worship service instead of the one for whom the worship service is created.

Have we been scattered and have we left Jesus alone by not seeing His providential care for us? Do we not see God at work in our circumstances? Dark times are allowed and come to us through the sovereignty of God. Are we prepared to let God do what He wants with us? Are we prepared to be separated from the outward, evident blessings of God? Until Jesus Christ is truly our Lord, we each have goals of our own which we serve. Our faith is real, but it is not yet permanent. And God is never in a

---

[107] Chambers, Oswald. "My Utmost for His Highest." Thomas Nelson Inc. (Utmost.org) http://utmost.org/fountains-of-blessings/ (accessed February 2, 2017).

hurry. If we are willing to wait, we will see God pointing out that we have been interested only in His blessings, instead of in God Himself. The sense of God's blessings is fundamental.[108]

Priorities are important. I remember a wise campus minister once telling me, "Barry, if Jesus is not first, chaos will exist in all other areas of your life." He was right. What are some of the signs that Jesus is not the Lord of our lives...

in our families?

_____

_____

_____

in our work?

_____

_____

_____

in our churches?

_____

_____

_____

---

[108] Chambers, Oswald. "My Utmost for His Highest."
http://utmost.org/fountains-of-blessings/

in our worship of God as a lifestyle?

_____

_____

_____

Deitrich Bonhoeffer lived from 1906-1945. With Bonhoeffer, context is everything. Bonhoeffer lived in WWII Nazi-occupied Europe. He was a marked man because he chose to stand up for his Christian faith and the Jewish Holocaust. As Nazism began to take over top church leadership posts in Germany in the mid 1930's, Bonhoeffer eventually chose to move to London. Later, he would return to Germany and help the resistance against the Nazis. He was eventually executed by the Nazis as Germany began to fall. In reading Bonhoeffer's material, we learn that persons who studied under Bonhoeffer in Nazi Germany were quickly ushered to the front lines of battle, often leading to their quick, untimely deaths. Even in the midst of overwhelming odds, Bonhoeffer maintained close contact with ministers who were persecuted in many and varied ways. In the dark days of World War II Germany, fellowship amongst the faithful was a real blessing.

> It is by the grace of God that a congregation is permitted to gather visibly in this world to share God's Word and sacrament. Not all Christians receive this blessing. The imprisoned, the sick, the scattered lonely, the proclaimers of the Gospel in heathen lands stand alone. They know that visible fellowship is a blessing.[109]

For most Christians in the western world, it is easy to put God first. It is our choice. Have you recently considered what a blessing it is to be able to worship God freely and openly without Christian persecution?

---

[109] Dietrich Bonhoeffer (1954) *Life Together* (New York: Harper & Row), 18.

_____

_____

_____

What are some persecutions that Christians are beginning to face in America and beyond? (Think about church shootings which are on the rise, how your church may no longer enjoy some of the benefits it once received from the government, and any other ways that may present themselves.)

_____

_____

_____

How are Christians around the world persecuted? (Iraq and Sudan come to mind as two areas where Christians are being killed for their faith.)

_____

_____

_____

How should we respond to persecution? (see 2 Corinthians 4:8-12, among other Scriptures)

_____

_____

_____

During suffering, blessings are more visible. I used to think that when I reached "the perfect place" in my life, it would be a place devoid of hardship, but now I realize that hardship and blessing go hand in hand. Think about reaching the top of Mount Everest. Many who tried have never reached the top of the mountain despite setting out. Some lost their lives. Others made it to the top. They accomplished their task with frostbite and painful joints from their arduous trek; it was not easy!

I think about the most beautiful sunrise in my lifetime. It was in Matamoras, Mexico. It contained pinks, blues, and white clouds in an amazing color pattern. Imagine what it would have looked like if the clouds were not there! The beauty would be absent. The clouds allow the sun's beauty to radiate in many colors as it rises above the horizon. Our lives are the same. Without conflict and hardship, we may not recognize real beauty when we see it. Tough times make great times even better! Uncle Henry Davis who died in 2005 used to say when it was raining, "Son, brighter days are coming!" He was right!

Bonhoeffer knew some of the greatest blessings imaginable, but they came not from being freed from a difficult situation. His blessings came from his relationship with the Lord that in turn gave him the strength to minister to others in the midst of life-threatening circumstances. Bonhoeffer's faith eventually cost him his life, but he was blessed every step of the way. I imagine that when Bonhoeffer faced death at the hands of the Nazis, he was thinking, "Heaven awaits! Glory to God."

C.S. Lewis (1898-1963)

"When we lose one blessing, another is often most unexpectedly given in its place."[110]

You've heard all of the cliches such as "When God closes a door, another one opens" or "When God closes a door, he opens a

---

[110] Lewis, C. S. (2008) Yours Jack (Zondervan), quote reprinted via http://www.deseretnews.com/top/817/57/Blessings-Top-100-CS-Lewis-quotes-.html (accessed February 2, 2017).

window." I remember them coming at some of the most inopportune times of my life. While we often do not want to hear such cliches, in the kingdom of God they are especially true.

I am a big fan of Garth Brooks, especially his early years when he was just starting his career. One of my favorite Garth songs is "Unanswered Prayers." While I believe that God always answers our prayers, I also believe that many times we are better off when God does not give us exactly what we desire. Whether when we lose our job, a relationship ends, or some other life circumstance occurs, it may be very painful. But God is often grooming us for an even greater reward that we could not have foreseen had we stayed in our current situation.

Life is a great reward, and we should willingly accept that God's ways are not our ways nor are his plans our plans. He wants to bless us with even larger blessings than we can imagine, but he can do so only if we let go of what we want and live into God's perfect and pleasing will for our lives.

Consider the birds of the air. Matthew 6:26-27 (NRSV) says, "Look at the birds of the air; they neither sow nor reap nor gather into barns, and yet your heavenly Father feeds them. Are you not of more value than they? And can any of you by worrying add a single hour to your span of life?"[111] They do not know where their next meal is coming from, but they do know that God will provide the blessing of another meal for them. They cannot see around the next bend or into the future, but God provides their next meal. The message is a simple but profound one; rather than trusting in what we see and in that which we think we can control, trust in God as he is the only one who will never disappoint.

I am reminded of Ecclesiastes. The author says, "Meaningless, utterly meaningless!"[112] in describing this life. And while he does go on to clarify what meaningless means later in the book, it is clear that great futility exists in anything we put stock in that is not God. While I have a hard time thinking that my family and friendships are meaningless, compared to the surpassing value

---

[111] Matthew 6:26-27, (NIV)
[112] Ecclesiastes 1:2, (NIV)

of knowing Jesus Christ as my Lord and Savior, everything is meaningless.

How do you apply Lewis' short but profound quote about blessings to your life?

_____

_____

_____

RECEIVE PRAYER REQUESTS BEFORE JOINING IN UNISON IN THE CLOSING PRAYER:

Dear Lord, thank you for the recent giants of the Christian faith who continue to teach us by their words. May we take to heart the ways in which they were blessed and apply their blessings to our own lives. Show us how to be grateful for the opportunity to worship you freely and openly. We pray for those experiencing Christian persecution that your hedge of protection may be over them and us. Help us to remember that when one blessing is taken away, another is soon to follow. We commit to putting you first in every area of our lives. Thank you for your great love for us. In Jesus' name, AMEN.

HOMEWORK: READ SESSION NINE AND WRITE DOWN YOUR ANSWERS TO THE QUESTIONS FOR GROUP DISCUSSION BEFORE THE NEXT GROUP SESSION

www.TheBlessedLifeBook.com

SECTION THREE

How Can I Bless Others?

SESSION NINE

How to Bless Your Spouse

OPEN THE BIBLE STUDY SESSION WITH PRAYER. ASK GOD TO BLESS YOUR TIME TOGETHER.

ANSWER THE QUESTIONS FOR GROUP DISCUSSION BELOW

In the series finale of *Magnum P.I.*, I will never forget what Tom Selleck said as he narrated the opening of the show. He said, "We all have a need inside of us to be loved." How true! We search after love day in and day out. Some of us successfully find it for a lifetime. Others of us find it for a time. But, the truth is that unless our marriage is centered in God in Christ Jesus, even though we love, our marriage may last for only a season.

How do we find a love that never ends? How do we form a marriage that is divorce-proof? I believe that the key to a long, healthy, stable marriage is found in our willingness to bless our spouse continually. How do we bless our spouse? Let's talk about several key points.

Bless Your Spouse by Praying with Your Spouse Daily

Did you know that marriages in which the couple prays with each other every day have only a one percent chance of divorce? Couples who pray together, stay together. Sadly, only four percent of all Christian couples pray together daily. Pastoral couples do slightly better as six percent. Why do we not pray together more often if prayer is that important?

In their article "Why People Don't Pray," Richard Hansen and David Wall discuss factors that come in the way of our prayer lives. They say that social psychologists have identified four questions at the heart of either doing something or having resistance to it.

1) Will it work for me?

For years Susan had kept her "daily appointment with God." Then her 10-year-old son was hit by a car. After hanging on for two weeks, he died. Susan now says, "What's the use of praying? I prayed harder in those two weeks than in my whole life, but Timmy still died!"
Susan no longer has confidence that prayer makes a difference. Her outcome expectations have been shaken. She knows how to pray but expects nothing to come from it.
How can Susan be helped? Since her prayer problems center on expectations, Susan needs guidance to see if what she expects prayer to accomplish is realistic and biblical. She might find, for example, that she has taken one aspect of prayer, petition, and isolated it from others, such as submission, intimacy, and comfort (as in Jesus' prayer in the Garden).[113]

How do we rekindle prayer in our lives when a tragic life event makes us question whether or not prayer really works? (see Psalm 17:1-6)

_____

_____

_____

Can you imagine what this must have been like for Susan? I think of many couples throughout the years and how a tragic loss like this might take them away from their prayer lives and ultimately God. Jean Galica says that one of the common myths of

---

[113] Hansen, Richard. "Why People Don't Pray." ChristianityToday.com http://www.christianitytoday.com/pastors/1994/fall/4l4061.html (accessed February 2, 2017).

marriage is that it will end in divorce if the death of a child occurs:

> One of the most commonly held myths is that after the death of a child, the majority of marriages end in divorce. The actual facts bear out that the death of a child usually acts, instead, to polarize the existing factors found in the marriage; hence, some marriage get worse, some get better, some just maintain, and some actually do end in divorce. Marriages that have sustained the loss of a child through death experience the same valleys and peaks as any other marriage, just in a more exaggerated form. Whether they become better or worse, the one sure thing is that the marriage will never be the same again as it was before the child's death.[114]

If life's trials and struggles amplify conflict in marriage, how do we reinforce our marriage so that we can make it through when trials and struggles come our way?

_____

_____

_____

We must work on blessing each other with the gift of prayer WELL BEFORE we hit turbulence in our marriages … no matter how large or small the turbulence may be. If we have a healthy marriage, the turbulence will serve to bring us closer together. If we have a weak marriage heading into a traumatic event, the event will serve to further weaken our marriage and thereby lead us to a possible divorce. Metaphorically, if we prepare for the storm before it comes, the damage done will be exponentially lessened.

---

[114] Galica, Jean. "The Effects of the Death of a Child on Marriage." Theravive.com http://www.theravive.com/research/The-Effects-of-the-Death-of-a-Child-on-a-Marriage (accessed February 2, 2017).

Do you remember the parable of "Building on the Solid Foundation"? When the streams rose, the man whose house was build on solid rock did not collapse because it had a firm foundation. The man who built his house on the sand lost his home because the wind and waves arose and caused the home to come down with a mighty crash (Matthew 7:24-27). The ultimate blessing we can give our marriages is the blessing of daily prayer together.

2) Can I Do It?

Frank became a Christian as an adult. He was enthusiastic about his faith, but when his pastor urged him to read the Bible each day, he thought, I've never liked to read. I don't even read the paper. Repeated challenges only made him feel defeated.

Frank's struggle is with self-efficacy--having confidence that he could successfully accomplish a task. Like the smoker who knows stopping will improve his health (outcome expectation) but doesn't think he has the willpower to quit (self-efficacy), Frank believes reading the Bible would help him grow spiritually, but that his nonliterary mindset leaves him powerless to read it regularly.

Several approaches can be taken to help Frank and those like him to increase their confidence. One is to link them with people of similar abilities and backgrounds who are mastering the task. A second is to provide them with small experiences of success, to build their skills and morale. A third is verbal encouragement.[115]

Have you ever heard a coach tell his quarterback to get in the game? Or, have you heard an Army General give orders so the troops know where to go and what to do? In the beginning, the quarterback and the troops have to learn how to do what is required of them. They have intense training to prepare them for the real

---

[115] Hansen, Richard. "Why People Don't Pray."

contest or conflict. Football players get hit again and again. Soldiers crawl through mud filled pits with bullets flying overhead. They do it willingly because they know they need the practice to be prepared for their adversaries. As Nike would say, "Just Do It!"

In our prayer lives, God wants us to pray together. At first, it may not come naturally and may feel awkward. In time, we cannot imagine life any other way. Can we do it? YES! Will we do it? That's a question that only we can answer!

Practice makes permanent. Will you commit to praying together with your spouse each day for the next two weeks? Be sure to ask your spouse if they are willing to pray with you. If they are hesitant, pray alone for your marriage until they join you. When praying together, journal the results after two weeks. How was your marriage before you began praying together? How is it now that you and your spouse are praying?

_____

_____

_____

3) What's It Worth to Me?

Joanie wonders if spending time "getting to know God," as her youth leader puts it, is a valuable goal in its own right. After all, she thinks to herself, I've enjoyed my life so far. How could spending time every day praying and reading the Bible make my life better?

Joanie is questioning the outcome value of personal devotions. She may already expect that it will make her a better Christian, and she may feel confident she could do it if she wanted to. But, she asks, why become a better Christian?

This may be the sleeper factor plaguing the

devotional life of many Christians. Of the four behavioral factors, it is the one most often overlooked. We assume that Christians would value the outcome of the spiritual disciplines, but outcomes are not valued unless they are defined, and that is not always easy to do. For example, what specific values are nurtured in the devotional life: A happier life? Closeness to God? Warm feelings? Insight into God's ways?

In Joanie's case, unless her youth pastor realizes that she does not see the value in personal devotions, the time spent encouraging devotional habits will be wasted. For someone to value spiritual disciplines may require nothing less than a call for spiritual renewal or conversion.[116]

I encourage all married couples to keep a journal of prayer requests and then to follow up on the requests to see how God has answered their prayers. It is true that if we believe that our prayers are hitting a wall, we start to ask ourselves, "Why pray?" But, I believe that our prayers hit a figurative wall only because we fail to recognize God's answers to our prayers. He may not answer them the way that we want, but God does answer our prayers. God is omnipotent (all powerful), omniscient (all-knowing), and omnipresent (everywhere at the same time). This means that God is right there with us when we pray. As a married couple, the challenge is to keep moving forward and to know that God is with us every step of the way.

Journaling is a great key to our prayer lives. Beyond journaling, what devotions can you and your spouse purchase at the Christian book store or online to read together? Keep it short!

_____

_____

_____

---

[116] Hansen, Richard. "Why People Don't Pray."

What will give you the fortitude to keep praying with your spouse even when it may seem that God is not hearing and answering your prayers as quickly as you may desire? (see 1 John 5:14)

_____

_____

_____

4) What will it cost me?

"What will I give up if I study this weekend?" asks Jeff. If it rains all weekend, the answer may be not much. But if it means missing a day at the beach with his girlfriend, the cost will be much higher. Jeff knows he can study effectively (self-efficacy), believes studying will result in good grades (outcome expectation) and realizes that good grades are important to his future (outcome value)--but he'd still rather go to the beach.

For personal devotions, cost is often expressed as "I don't have enough time." Sleep, recreation, family, and work schedules all compete for the heart and the mind.

How do we help people "count the cost," as Jesus counseled? One way is to strengthen the first three factors (expectations, skills, and values). As people see the worth of prayer and Bible reading, they become more willing to pay a higher cost.

Another approach is to lower the cost. For example, the novice, rather than being urged to practice a "sweet hour of prayer" each day, might be encouraged to spend five minutes a day in prayer and Bible reading.[117]

We've already discussed the enormous savings that come when a married couple prays together. The risk of divorce goes

---

[117] Hansen, Richard. "Why People Don't Pray."

down to 1% in a world where the divorce norm is above 50%. Eisenhower was a master of counting the cost in World War II. He realized that if the Army created a diversion, they could save lives. Eisenhower built a dummy army out of balloon tanks and jeeps so that Hitler would move the majority of his forces to where Hitler thought Eisenhower was going to land on D-Day. Eisenhower even sent General Patton to the "dummy" location just to ensure that Hitler bought it. What was the result? Many lives were lost on the beaches of Normandy, but hundreds of thousands were saved, and the Allies secured the beachhead in France. It became a foothold that allowed the Allies to win the war; they defeated Hitler.

Spousal prayer is our stronghold and fortress in marriage. With it, we can conquer any problem that we face because God is on our side. Without it, we are stuck in the sand or, worse yet, left to end our marriage because we see no other option. A wise friend once said something crucial to my marriage. She said, "Barry, are you willing to fight for your marriage?" We all need to fight for our marriages so that then (and only then) can we experience the blessed life within our marriages.

As you count the cost of prayer in your marriage, what might it cost you if you do not pray willingly and openly with your spouse?

_____

_____

_____

Bless Your Spouse by Finding Your Self-Worth in God and Not in Your Spouse

The Bible tells us of two dichotomies when thinking about our self-worth. The first is those who trust in other human beings for validity, confidence, and the ability to accomplish much in life. The second is those who look to God to provide for their lives. Jeremiah 17: 5-10 (NIV) says, "Cursed is the one who trusts in man, who draws strength from mere flesh and whose heart turns away from the Lord. That person will be like a bush in the wastelands; they will not see prosperity when it comes. They will dwell in the parched places of the desert, in a salt land where no one lives. But blessed is the one who trusts in the Lord, whose confidence is in him. They will be like a tree planted by the water that sends out its roots by the stream. it does not fear when heat comes; its leaves are always green. It has no worries in a year of drought and never fails to bear fruit."[118]

Where do you find your self-worth and self-esteem? Do you allow others to make you happy, sad, or angry? Is there anything you do just to obtain the approval of other people? Most of us at some point in our lives are guilty of looking to our parents, a teacher or mentor, a close friend, or a spouse for validation. We find our self-worth in what they think and say about us. How they treat us determines whether or not we may be happy or depressed.

The problem with such an approach is that it robs God of his rightful place as the caretaker of our souls. God in Christ Jesus is the only one who will never disappoint us or leave us. In marriage, the two should become one and our spouse should be our best friend, YES! But if we are always expecting our spouse to change to become the person that we need her to be for us to be happy, it will only lead to further misery for our spouse and us.

Hebrews 13:4-7 (NIV) says, "Marriage should be honored by all, and the marriage bed kept pure, for God will judge the adulterer and all the sexually immoral. Keep your lives free from the love of money and be content with what you have, because God has said, 'Never will I leave you; never will I forsake you.' So we say with confidence, 'The Lord is my helper; I will not be afraid. What can mere mortals do to me?' Remember your leaders, who spoke the word of God to you. Consider the outcome of their way of life and imitate their

---

[118] Jeremiah 17: 5-10, (NIV)

faith." [119]

Hebrews 13 states that husband and wife should be one in marriage; marriage starts and ends with God. God wants us to avoid materialism because it will only serve to complicate the marriage. He is always with us to bless our marriages as we seek Him. We should look to those who have healthy marriages and learn from them. Their life experiences (both good and bad) can help us to make our marriage better. We need to be open to seeking advice and wise counsel before the marriage derails or is stuck in a rut. As one person once told me, "Don't wait until your marriage is stuck in the ditch (metaphor of a car stuck in the ditch). Seek wise counsel and help early on during a bump in the road or a stumbling block so that it does not become a full-blown crisis." Another person once said, "If you want my help, do not invite me to the site where the plane has already crashed. Invite me to be a part of the process while the plane is still circling the airport so that we can have a safe landing." We all face difficulties in marriage. The important thing is how we respond when crises arise.

Think about it this way. My wife, Erin, and I are two very different people. We both have taken the Leading From Your Strengths personality assessment tool (found at ministryinsights.com) which centers on four different behavioral traits. Each personality trait is represented by an animal. She is an off-the-charts Otter and I am a Golden Retriever / Beaver. Her core life motto would be: "I want our marriage to be fun!" She walks into a room and is immediately the life of the party. My core life motto would be: "I just want us to love each other!" In our case, opposites attract. In reality, it can make for turbulence in our marriage.

One of my love languages (based on Gary Chapman's *Five Love Languages* -- it is still well worth the read!) is Words of Affirmation. Erin does not naturally praise me. She will walk into a room that I spent how painting and she will say, "You missed a spot!" At the beginning of our marriage, I

---

was greatly offended because my loving personality was thinking, "Doesn't she care that I just painted this whole room and now she is offending me by noticing the one little blip in the sea of perfection?!" Well, she did not care and she just wanted the one little spot to be painted.

As I have grown in our marriage, I have come to realize Erin is who God made her to be and God created me just as he wanted me. I should not expect Erin to change just because she is married to me. We both need to find our completeness and wholeness in God before we ever come together as a married couple. God is the glue that holds us together. Any other understanding of our marriage could lead to constant disagreements and arguments-- or worse yet, divorce.

Erin is getting better about pointing out the one item that is wrong when I am working hard to do something. I now do not take it so personally. She can appreciate the handyman that God created me to be as I appreciate the person who will always be brutally honest with me. Humorously, I now ask Erin how my sermons were after I deliver them on Sunday mornings. I now recognize that if I can get a sermon past her, it must have been a good one.

Where do you go to find your self-worth? Isaiah 43:1-4 (NIV) says, "But now, this is what the Lord says— he who created you, Jacob, he who formed you, Israel: 'Do not fear, for I have redeemed you; I have summoned you by name; you are mine. When you pass through the waters, I will be with you; and when you pass through the rivers, they will not sweep over you. When you walk through the fire, you will not be burned; the flames will not set you ablaze. For I am the Lord your God, the Holy One of Israel, your Savior; I give Egypt for your ransom, Cush and Seba in your stead. Since you are precious and honored in my sight, and because I love you, I will give people in exchange for you, nations in exchange for your life'".[120]

Find your self-worth in God alone and then come together with your spouse. You'll conclude that it will make marriage

---

[120] Isaiah 43:1-4, (NIV)

much more enjoyable. It will be a blessed marriage, able to stand the test of time.

What is the danger of finding our self worth in our marriage and not first in God?

_____

_____

_____

Where do you currently find your self worth? Take a brief inventory and adjust your life accordingly.

_____

_____

_____

Bless Your Spouse by Putting Your Spouse's Needs Above Your Own

In *Secrets to a Happy Marriage: Putting Your Spouse First*, author Mel Robbins gives several insights as to why we should put our spouse's needs above our own:

First, a strong marriage is the healthiest thing you can give your kids. Your kids feel safe and loved when they see two parents who work as a team, take interest in each other, make an effort, display both respect and affection and act like one another's favorite, even after all these years.

Second, if you put your spouse first, your marriage will last your lifetime. If you want your marriage to last your lifetime, give it the attention and effort it deserves.

Your kids will live with you for just two short decades. Putting your marriage on cruise control for 20 years, while you focus on your kids is like falling asleep at the wheel – deadly. When your kids leave, your spouse is the one who's left.

Third, spouses aren't roommates, they're partners and lovers. When your kids become the center of your universe … your role as [spouse] gets shelved. Slowly you start to feel like a taxi driver, lunch packer and homework checker. You and your spouse become so busy focusing on everything but each other that you drift apart. At first you just feel really busy, but then you start to feel like roommates. You settle into that routine assuming it's a phase. And you're right it is a phase: – it's the beginning of the end. Suddenly the kids are gone – and you can't remember why you married each other in the first place.

Fourth, you don't want to raise obnoxious kids: When you make kids the center of your universe, they turn into adults who think they are the center of the universe.

Fifth, don't you want your kids to grow up and marry someone who puts them first? Of course you do! And, it's your job to teach them what it looks like. Show them with your marriage first.[121]

Scripture backs up this need to put our spouse before ourselves and before our children. Proverbs 20:6-7 (NIV) says, "Many claim to have unfailing love, but a faithful person who can find? The righteous lead blameless lives; blessed are their children after them."[122] In other words, the ultimate blessing for our children is to put our spouse first. A stable home is a great key to a child's future success.

Philippians 2:3 (NIV) further supports the need to put others before ourselves: "Do nothing from rivalry or conceit, but in humility count others more significant than yourselves."

[121] Robbins, Mel. "Secret to a Happy Marriage: Put Your Spouse First." Success.com http://www.success.com/blog/secret-to-a-happy-marriage-put-your-spouse-first (accessed February 2, 2017).
[122] Proverbs 20:6-7, (NIV)

[123] This Scripture is telling us that selflessness is desireable. Our own agenda and self-motivated ambition must take second seat to having a strong, vibrant marriage that is blessed by God.

How can you work with your spouse to make sure adjustments are made that will be mutually beneficial to both you and your spouse? How can you bless your spouse this week by putting her needs before your own?

Do you put your spouse before yourself? Why or why not? (What would your spouse say if asked them candidly?)

_____

_____

_____

Do you put your spouse before your children? Why or why not? (Again, what would your spouse say? Be honest!)

_____

_____

_____

What can be the danger of putting our spouse beneath ourselves and our children on our priorities list?

_____

_____

_____

---

[123] Philippians 2:3, (NIV)

Here are a few suggestions on how you can put your spouse before yourself:

- Bring him/her coffee every morning.
- Hug, hold hands, often.
- Text/flirt throughout the day (reminders "just thinking about you xo")
- Make your bedroom a no-kids zone – explain to the kids that it's "your space."
- Say I love you, in front of the kids, daily.
- Plan the week as a family, every Sunday, to make logistics a minimum.[124]

Blessing your spouse is not impossible. In fact, it is a lot easier than you may think. It requires intentionality to do the right things so that you can have a marriage that will flourish. We all have a limited amount of time and energy. We must stop doing what brings stagnation in marriage and start doing what will bring blessing today! It's never too late to start blessing your spouse.

What are a few steps you can take to bless your spouse this week (either listed above or items beyond these)?

_____

_____

_____

RECEIVE PRAYER REQUESTS BEFORE JOINING IN UNISON IN THE CLOSING PRAYER:

Dear Lord, thank you for your great love for me. Thank you for my spouse. Give me the love with which to love my spouse daily and to see my spouse as you see them. Show

---

124 Robbins, Mel. "Secret to a Happy Marriage: Put Your Spouse First."

me how to fall more in love with my spouse daily. Give me wisdom to put you first, my spouse second, and my children third in my priorities. Strengthen my prayer life as it keeps my spouse and me connected to you and one another. In Jesus' name, AMEN.

HOMEWORK: READ SESSION TEN AND WRITE DOWN YOUR ANSWERS TO THE QUESTIONS FOR GROUP DISCUSSION BEFORE THE NEXT GROUP SESSION

www.TheBlessedLifeBook.com

SESSION TEN

How to Bless Your Children

OPEN THE BIBLE STUDY SESSION WITH PRAYER. ASK
GOD TO BLESS YOUR TIME TOGETHER.

ANSWER THE QUESTIONS FOR GROUP DISCUSSION
BELOW

I remember the time just before Erin and I became
parents. We were newlyweds fresh out of the gate of marriage.
We were married for five months before we found out that we
were pregnant with our first child. While it was a miscarriage,
it opened the floodgates for us to want a child. We were then
ready to pursue all that God had for us in parenting and to
realize the absence that we felt with the loss of our first
pregnancy. Now we are blessed with a large family. Each day
is full of surprises as we raise our children. We believe each
child is a gift from God. Our children challenge us each day in
many ways, including with the responsibility that we possess
to raise them well so that one day they will be adults "after
God's own heart."

I was raised in a household where saying the words "I
love you" was seldom if ever heard. I even remember one
Sunday at our church in Cairo the preacher challenged us to
tell others "I love you." My grandfather, a great Christian
man, looked over at me and said, "Barry, I appreciate you." It
meant a lot, but I also wanted to hear those three words, "I love
you." I do not fault my grandfather for not saying those words.
Later in college, I took the opportunity to initiate it and he
responded, "I love you too." I still remember where I was as I
talked on the phone with him that day.

Many families do not say "I love you" because it is not
ingrained in the historical culture of their family. We live in a
world where love is defined in such wrong ways that we need
to be the flag bearers who take it upon ourselves to define love

properly; love should always be God-centered and unconditional. We have an obligation for our children to see us taking the lead in sharing love in the right ways. The ways we raise our children will determine the values that they pass on to their children in the future.

Loving our children is a God-sized task and is one of the greatest ways we can bless our children. It is a parent's responsibility to bless his children. We must be careful to keep it positive. When we are overly critical, it can foster seeds in the life of our children that lead them to make poor decisions in the future. They may lack self-confidence and self-worth because we never built them up in the virtues of God. It is essential that we share words with our children that will inspire them to reach their highest potential. God wants us to inspire and motivate them (with His help) to do their absolute best each day. This includes telling our children how proud we are of them on a frequent basis. Tell your child, "I am so proud of you because you are my child and are doing great things." It may not seem like a great deal to us, but it may be the difference between a blessed child and a child with a small or missing sense of self-worth in the world. Like it or not, children often think of value and self-worth through the eyes of their parents. A parent's highest calling is to value their children and ultimately help his children to be complete in his relationship with Jesus Christ.

Do you tell your children "I love you" freely and openly? Why or why not? Do you wait until they tell you or do you share it frequently? (see 1 Corinthians 13)

_____

_____

_____

Do you tell your children how proud you are of them? Is it

136

conditional (based on what they do) or are you proud of them just because they are your child?

_____

_____

_____

Defining the Word "Blessing" as It Relates to Our Children

But what exactly *is* a blessing?

Consider this contrast. No parent hopes his child grows up to be a failure. Our love wants nothing but health, happiness, and God's best for each of them. A blessing is simply a God-ordained way to handle these loving desires for our children, turning them from hopeful wishes into future realities.

To bless someone actually means that we speak well of him. It is a parent's God-given responsibility to verbally affirm his children for who they are, while also encouraging and inspiring them toward future success.

In a blessing, powerful words and wishes combine with prayers and praise. God instructed Moses to teach the high priests how to bless the sons of Israel. "Say to them: 'The LORD bless you, and keep you; the LORD make His face shine on you, and be gracious to you; the LORD lift up His countenance on you, and give you peace.' So they shall invoke My name on the sons of Israel, and I then will bless them" (Numbers 6:24-27).

Pointing out a child's skill or character could be part of a blessing. Say things like: "I could see you becoming a great ..." or "With your strengths and abilities, you could probably ..." or "What impresses me is your giftedness and heart for ..."[125]

How can you bless your child this week?

_____

_____

_____

Speaking the Blessings of God Over Our Children

Recently, I read an article that conveys that sense of blessing that we want to convey to our children. When we bless our children, we should invoke the very presence of God.

Listed below are the most commonly referenced compound names of Jehovah, the trait of His person to which each refers and a suggestion of how to use the name:

Jehovah-Jireh: The Lord Our Provider (see Gen. 22:14): Speak a blessing in the face of specific need, whatever realm the need may represent.

Jehovah-Raah: The Lord Our Shepherd (see Ps. 23:1): Speak a blessing with the reminder of God's never-forsaking presence and protection.

Jehovah-Shalom: The Lord Our Peace (see Judg. 6:24): Speak a blessing that will comfort in the midst of turmoil or upset.

Jehovah-Rapha: The Lord Our Healer (see Ex. 15:26): Speak a blessing that calls for God's grace of healing, knowing that He wants to heal the sick.

---

[125] Kenrick, Alex and Stephen. "Are Your Blessing Your Children." FamilyLife.com "http://www.familylife.com/articles/topics/parenting/foundations/spiritual-development/are-you-blessing-your-children (accessed February 3, 2017).

Jehovah-Nissi: The Lord Our Victory (see Ex. 17:15): Speak a blessing that reminds the child that the battle is not theirs but the Lord's.

Jehovah-Tsidkenu: The Lord Our Righteousness (see Ps. 23:3): Speak a blessing that declares how justice (righteousness) will come from God, even when unfair circumstances seem to be dominating.

Jehovah-Shammah: The Lord Is Present (see Ezek. 48:35): Speak a blessing that deepens the assurance of the Lord's attendant care and keeping presence.

As you bless, always see that your demeanor conveys the spirit and heart of our loving, living God. He not only wants to bless that child, but He also has called you and me to accept the responsibility for directly *inviting* that blessing.[126]

Alex and Stephen Kendrick say, "After Jesus was baptized, a voice came from heaven: "You are My beloved Son, in You I am well-pleased" (Mark 1:11). God the Father publicly affirmed and blessed His Son, and then invested in Jesus' future success by immediately sending His Holy Spirit to fill Him (Luke 3:22). This powerful experience set Jesus up to completely fulfill the will of His heavenly Father during His earthly ministry."[127]

Do you speak God's blessings upon your child? Do you speak well of your child when talking with others?

---

[126] Hayford, Jack. "How to Effectively Speak Blessings Upon Your Children." CharismaMag.com
http://www.charismamag.com/life/family-parenting/15245-speaking-blessings-upon-your-children (accessed February 3, 2017).

[127] Kendrick, Alex and Stephen. "Are You Blessing Your Children?" FamilyLife.com
http://www.familylife.com/articles/topics/parenting/foundations/spiritual-development/are-you-blessing-your-children (accessed March 27, 2017).

Praying for our Children to Be Blessed

How is your prayer life? Do you pray over your children daily? Perhaps this is one of the most profound ways we can bless our children, through the power of prayer. Jon Bloom gives us seven specific helpful ways that we can pray over our children:

1. That Jesus will call them and no one will hinder them from coming.

Then children were brought to him that he might lay his hands on them and pray. The disciples rebuked the people, but Jesus said, "Let the little children come to me and do not hinder them, for to such belongs the kingdom of heaven." And he laid his hands on them and went away.(Matthew 19:13–15)

2. That they will respond in faith to Jesus's faithful, persistent call.

The Lord is not slow to fulfill his promise as some count slowness, but is patient toward you, not wishing that any should perish, but that all should reach repentance. (2 Peter 3:9)

3. That they will experience sanctification through the transforming work of the Holy Spirit and will increasingly desire to fulfill the greatest commandments.

And he said to him, "You shall love the Lord your God with all your heart and with all your soul and with all your mind. This is the great and first commandment. And a second is like it: You shall love your neighbor as yourself." (Matthew 22:37-39)

4. That they will not be unequally yoked in intimate relationships, especially marriage.

Do not be unequally yoked with unbelievers. For what partnership has righteousness with lawlessness? Or what fellowship has light with darkness? (2 Corinthians 6:14)
5. That their thoughts will be pure.
Finally, brothers, whatever is true, whatever is honorable, whatever is just, whatever is pure, whatever is lovely, whatever is commendable, if there is any excellence, if there is anything worthy of praise, think about these things. (Philippians 4:8)
6. That their hearts will be stirred to give generously to the Lord's work.
All the men and women, the people of Israel, whose heart moved them to bring anything for the work that the Lord had commanded by Moses to be done brought it as a freewill offering to the Lord. (Exodus 35:29)
7. That when the time is right, they will GO!
And Jesus came and said to them, "All authority in heaven and on earth has been given to me. Go therefore and make disciples of all nations, baptizing them in the name of the Father and of the Son and of the Holy Spirit, teaching them to observe all that I have commanded you. And behold, I am with you always, to the end of the age." (Matthew 28:18-20)[128]

Do you pray for your children daily? (see Job 42:10)

_____

_____

_____

How can you give a blessing to your child?

[128] Bloom, Jon. "Seven Things to Pray for Your Children." DesiringGod.org http://www.desiringgod.org/articles/seven-things-to-pray-for-your-children (accessed Feburary 3, 2017).

Dr. John Trent and Dr. Gary Smalley outlined five biblical steps for giving a blessing to children in their book *The Blessing: Meaningful Touch, A Spoken Message, Attaching High Value, Picturing a Special Future, and An Active Commitment.* I have expanded on these steps below.

1. *Meaningful Touch.* Before a word is spoken, there should be the laying on of hands, a hug, or a reaching out to touch. We see this throughout Scripture, both in the Old and New Testaments. Appropriate touch conveys in powerful, nonverbal ways our love and affirmation. Touch prepares the way for our words.

2. *A Spoken Message.* In biblical times, children weren't left to "fill in the blanks" as to whether they were valuable to a parent or grandparent. Words were used, aloud and in writing. Today, words can place unconditional love and acceptance into the heart of a child or loved one.

3. *Attaching High Value.* But what words do you say or write? The word blessing carries the idea that the person you're blessing is of incredible worth and value, even as an imperfect person. In short, you're helping a child get the picture that you see things in his or her life today that make the child special, useful, and of great value to you.

4. *Picturing a Special Future.* With our touch and with our words that attach high value, the response in our children's or loved ones' hearts can be nothing short of transformational. The light goes on in their hearts and minds when they realize that, because of the way God made them, they can do more than they ever dreamed in living out a God-honoring future.

5. *An Active Commitment.* Blessing children doesn't mean we never discipline them or point out areas where growth is needed. But children know at an incredibly deep level if they have their parents' blessing—if their mom or dad, grandmother, aunt, uncle, or other loved one really sees high value in them—even during the tough times. Genuine commitment is an unconditional commitment to an

imperfect person that says as long as I have breath, I'll be there to see to build these five elements of blessing into your life story.[129]

Which of these five items can you put into practice this week? How will you do it?

_____

_____

_____

Putting Your Child Into the Service of the Almighty

I can fathom no greater blessing than allowing your child to serve the Lord. Scripture is full of examples of generational blessings that came as the parents of a child were obedient to the Lord by placing the child in his service. Abraham was obedient to the Lord by being prepared to sacrifice Isaac on the altar. God spared Isaac because of Abraham's obedience. Isaac's place in the lineage of blessed families was forever cemented. Jesse offered up David for service as king. It's interesting that when Samuel picked David, Jesse wanted to give Samuel another son because David was the smallest of all his boys. Hannah offered Samuel into the service of the Lord even before he was born. God granted her wish to have a child. To fulfill her promise to God, she took him to serve in the priestly court at a young age with Eli. Tons of other examples include John the Baptist, Jesus, and others.

Are you willing to pray daily for God's will to be done in your child's life? Will you accept God's will for your child's life even if it is different from the vision you have for your child's future?

_____

---

[129] Anthony, Michelle. (2015) *Becoming a Spiritually Healthy Family: Avoiding the Six Dysfunctional Parenting Styles.* (Colorado Springs, CO: David C. Cook), 115–116.

I could go on and on, but the point is simple. It is my belief that for far too long, the family unit has abandoned to the church faith education and teaching. "Well, let the church teach my child about how to know Jesus as their Lord and Savior!" While the church does indeed need to be a place of sharing Jesus and making disciples, faith should start at home. From the youngest of ages, mom and dad should take the awesome responsibility not just to provide for their children in physical and emotional ways, but also spiritually. Does it mean that every child has to be a priest or Pope? No! But it does mean that every parent takes the responsibility to raise his child in faith even before the child is born. Being a parent is an awesome responsibility, and parents should understand their responsibility at the moment of conception, not at the moment of a conflict or problem in the life of their child.

Having kids is great fun! Paxton and I love to hang Christmas lights together each year. I love to watch Maddux as he builds the newest Lego creation or as he plays a video game that he loves. Lennox is my little wide-open man. He is sweet and tough, all rolled into one. Raising our children is a challenge. I have a responsibility to raise them in the Lord and to bless them daily. One day, they may choose their own path. I may like or dislike their path. If they choose a path outside of God's will, it will not be because I did not show them Jesus or try to give them God's blessings each day. Teaching faith and blessing our children starts at home. Check out ItStartsAtHome.org. Steve Stroope and his team have done an amazing job of creating resources to help bring faith back into our homes.

Do you accept the responsibility to nurture your child in the faith daily? Why or why not? (see Proverbs 22:6)

_____

_____

_____

RECEIVE PRAYER REQUESTS BEFORE JOINING IN
UNISON IN THE CLOSING PRAYER:

**Dear Lord, thank you for loving me. Thank you for my
children and the blessing they are to me. Show me how to
bless my children daily. I want to be the parent you have
created me to be and to teach my children about you. Give
me the strength to endure hardship and the ability to
praise you for the joy my children bring to me. Every good
and perfect gift is from you, and my children are truly a
gift. In Jesus' name, AMEN.**

HOMEWORK: READ SESSION ELEVEN AND WRITE DOWN
YOUR ANSWERS TO THE QUESTIONS FOR GROUP
DISCUSSION BEFORE THE NEXT GROUP SESSION

www.TheBlessedLifeBook.com

SESSION ELEVEN

The Power of the Written Blessing

OPEN THE BIBLE STUDY SESSION WITH PRAYER. ASK
GOD TO BLESS YOUR TIME TOGETHER.

ANSWER THE QUESTIONS FOR GROUP DISCUSSION
BELOW

Consider this: The earliest writing of which we are aware
began when symbols were scratched or pressed on clay tablets.
The Egyptians refined this technique and developed an early form
of writing known as hieroglyphics. The Bible tells us that Moses
was "educated in all the learning of the Egyptians," so he would
have been familiar with the major writing systems of his time. We
read that God gave Moses "two tablets of the Testimony, the
tablets of stone inscribed by the finger of God"(Exodus 31:18). All
this leads to the conclusion that the earliest writings in the Bible
were set down around 1400 BC.[130]

Now consider the use of the printing press during the time
of Johann Gutenberg. Gutenberg lived from 1398-1468. He was
highly skilled in the use of sheet metal, molds, and ink that allowed
for the creation of the Gutenberg Bible. For the first time in
history, monks and scribes did not hold the keys to replicating new
copies of God's word. Mass quantities were produced, and the
Bible became widely available for priests and more ordinary
people. While literacy to that point in society was limited to a
small group, the Bible encouraged literacy to spread and eventually
led to the translation of the Bible into multiple languages. Biblical
literacy, in turn, fueled the Protestant Reformation.[131]

---

[130] "When was the Bible Written?" The International Bible Society - Biblica.com
http://www.biblica.com/bible/bible-faqs/when-was-the-bible-written/ (accessed February 3,
2017).

[131] "1456: Gutenburg Produces the First Printed Bible." ChristiantyToday.com
http://www.christianitytoday.com/history/issues/issue-28/1456-gutenberg-produces-first-prin
ted-bible.html (accessed February 3, 2017).

The written word of God fueled the Christian movement, both in 1400 BC and in the 15th century AD. How important is it for us to continue to distribute the written word of God in our churches and around the world? (see Hebrews 4:12)

_____

_____

_____

What happens when people do not know the word of God but try to share the Good News of Jesus Christ? (see 2 Peter 2:1)

_____

_____

_____

What types of false prophets exist in the present day?

_____

_____

_____

Written words last long after the author writes it. That is why we must be careful with mediums such as Facebook and Twitter because sometimes we write content in the heat of the moment that are damaging to us and others for a long time to come. Employers now check social media accounts before offering someone a job. If the person interviewed well but has a social media account the employer does not like, a job offer may not be given. Many say that John Wesley never had a thought that he did not write down. It is probably one of the greatest reasons that we remember him so well in the present day. He was indeed a giant of his time as his revival movement led to political stability that allowed England to escape the European revolutions relatively unscathed. But his writings were what endured. We see brilliance in how he spoke of his theology and ministry that have allowed many a preacher to define their theological beliefs since Wesley first wrote his words between 1703 and 1791. The written word endures, and it can either build up or tear down.

Think about your Facebook posts, e-mails, and speech. Does it build up others or tear down? As you think about the group discussion, what posts have you viewed on Facebook that may have changed your opinions of an individual (both in positive and negative ways)?

_____

_____

_____

I encourage you to be someone who writes. If you do not write books, you can write notes to other people. A note is an excellent way to bless the life of someone else simply by your expression of caring through the written word. A note is something that many others will place on their refrigerator or cabinet and come back to again and again. It symbolizes to the receiver that someone else cared enough to take the time to write it. It shows that we are thinking about them. In a world in which everyone is going to e-mail and texts, it is important that the note is handwritten. I can shoot out a thousand emails in a short period, yes; however, a handwritten note takes time for me to write which in turn adds value for the recipient. It is a fountain of blessing that blesses both the writer and receiver again and again.

Are you currently someone who writes handwritten notes? How

do you feel when you receive a handwritten note?

_____

_____

_____

What types of handwritten notes should we write?

1) Make It Personal:

I took to the Scriptures to help me learn more about the importance of the handwritten note. In 2 Thessalonians 3:17, Colossians 4:18, 1 Corinthians 16:21, and Philemon 1:19, Paul says a similar word, "I, Paul, write this greeting in my own hand." He did not section it out for someone else to do. He did it himself! That became a great way for the early church to realize that Paul was in it with them. Paul longed to be with them and to do ministry with them. It made the early church much more steadfast in their own resolve.

2) Remember Your Audience:

A wise man once shared some advice with me. He said that it does not matter what message I am trying to communicate. It matters more what the hearer is going to hear when I deliver my message. I may have the best advice in the all the world. But if it is ill-timed or it falls on deaf ears, my message is wasted. My words could cause harm.

Paul knew this well. In Acts 23:6, Paul says that he is a Pharisee from a family of Pharisees. Pharisees were some of the most strict Jews of their day. They practiced all of the Jewish customs with vigilance. And yet, when he writes, he writes in Galatians 5:2 (NIV), "Mark my words! I, Paul, tell you that if you let yourselves be circumcised, Christ will be of no value to you at all."[132]

For Paul to say that circumcision is not essential to the believer's relationship with God was revolutionary. Up to that point, all Jews had to be circumcised to have a relationship with God. Paul was laying down a new law from God, especially because his hearers of the written word would be Gentiles, those who were not Jewish from birth. Not having to be circumcised was an essential message for the Gentiles to hear, because it removed an obstacle that kept them from believing in Jesus freely and openly.

Would Paul write the same letters to the Jews he was seeking to convert to Christianity? I believe his message would be very different. He would focus more on a relationship with Jesus Christ. While circumcision was an obstacle to belief for Gentiles, it was not a problem for Jews because they were already circumcised.

When I communicate with my young children, I communicate differently than I would with an older adult. Does it mean that the message changes? No. But, how I communicate that message makes all the difference in whether or not the message is received.

3) Be a Blessing and Not A Curse

We live in a sad day and age where teenage online bullying has led to a new phenomena of teenagers taking their lives. The teenager may have never met the bully face to face and does not know the bully's real life personality. Other times, the teenager knows the bully from school. The bully uses indirect references to belittle the teenager and cause emotional harm. The words the bully writes are like daggers to the heart of a young boy or girl. It reminds me that the old phrase is incorrect that says "sticks and stones may break my bones but words will never hurt me." Words do hurt. Words can build up or tear down in an instant. We need to be on the end of history that seeks to make the life of someone else better and not worse.

---

[132] Galatians 5:2, (NIV)

Scripture speaks to this many times. Deuteronomy 28: 1-5 (NIV) says, "If you fully obey the Lord your God and carefully follow all his commands I give you today, the Lord your God will set you high above all the nations on earth. All these blessings will come on you and accompany you if you obey the Lord your God: You will be blessed in the city and blessed in the country. The fruit of your womb will be blessed, and the crops of your land and the young of your livestock—the calves of your herds and the lambs of your flocks. Your basket and your kneading trough will be blessed."[133] The Lord commands us to "love [our] neighbors"[134] (Matthew 12:31, NIV) and to "pray for those who persecute [us]" (Matthew 5:44). In Luke 6:28 (NLT), it goes so far as to say, "Bless those who curse you. Pray for those who hurt you."[135] Proverbs 25:26 (NIV) drives this point home when it says, "Like a muddied spring or a polluted fountain is a righteous man who gives way before the wicked."[136]

God's goal for us is to be a blessing to others even when they curse us. Proverbs 11:25-26 (NIV) says, "Whoever brings blessing will be enriched, and one who waters will himself be watered. The people curse him who holds back grain, but a blessing is on the head of him who sells it."[137] Judgment is God's alone to take. Our job is to keep passing the problems and difficulties of this world onto God so that they do not lead us to the point where we desire to curse someone else.

How can we bless someone else with a written blessing?

Think about Numbers 6:24–26, which gives us the Aaronic blessing. This is the blessing Moses instructed his brother, Aaron, to place on the people of Israel. Thank God for it! When you try to improve on it, you realize you are not going to make much headway.

---

[133] Deuteronomy 28: 1-5, (NIV)

[134] Matthew 12:31, (NIV)

[135] Luke 6:28, (NLT)

[136] Proverbs 25:26, (NIV)

[137] Proverbs 11:25-26 (NIV)

"The Lord bless you." That means "God bring good consistently into your life." "The Lord bless you and keep you." That means "God protect you. God build around you his safekeeping. The blood of Jesus and the Spirit of Christ be over you and keep you." Stop for a moment and think about saying that to someone: "God bless you and keep you." Imagine looking them in the eyes when you say it. This is very intimate and can be threatening. I've done this with groups where people broke out in tears and broke out in laughter because it touched so deeply.

Emphasize you. This needs to be very personal. "God bless you and keep you. God make his face to shine upon you." There's so much about the face of God in the Bible. One of the most precious things that we can have is living before the shining face of God. Now, if you have trouble with the shining face, find a grandparent somewhere and watch their face shine on their grandchild; that can give you a little idea. There is such radiance that comes out of a person with the shining face. And your face is meant to shine. Glory is meant to be shared from God to human beings. Glory always shines.[138]

These words shared by Dallas Willard remind us of the importance of visualizing the person on the receiving end of the written blessing. I think about those people with whom I am angry from time to time. It is very hard for me to remain angry with them if I visualize them as a child of God and I pray God's blessings on them before I have a chance to interact with them again. Even the "thorns in my side" are God's blessings in disguise if I will allow God to use them to teach me something I needed to know. It is important for us to bless and not curse. Blessing others is a God-sized task!

4) Remember to say "Thank You!"

---

[138] Willard, Dallas. "The Right Way to Give Someone a Blessing.' ChristianityToday.com http://www.christianitytoday.com/ct/2014/january-february/right-way-to-give-someone-blessi ng.html (accessed February 3, 2017).

Saying "Thanks!" sounds counterintuitive, especially because we all remember writing "Thank You" notes for graduation gifts and wedding presents. I will never forget that writing thank-you notes was not my strong suit in high school. I received the lion's share of gifts. While I was grateful for presents received, I did not like to write the notes. In hindsight, I see that those people who gave me the gifts did so because they loved me dearly. I realize that the least that I could do was to be grateful for those expressions of love that they sent my way. My wife, Erin, wrote the vast majority of our wedding thank you notes. We were blessed beyond belief. While I did not write the majority of the notes, the names and faces that each gift represented truly helped me to understand better how loved we were and the value of great friendships and wholesome relationships.

Recently, I received a thank-you note that impacted me. Our new Bishop of the South Georgia Annual Conference sent me a thank-you note for the flowers that I sent him (on behalf of our church) when he moved in. My message on the flowers said that he was invited to preach any time and that we as a community of faith would be praying for him. It meant a great deal that the Bishop took the time to take his pen and send me a heartfelt thank you. We all were grateful for the thoughts that his note represented.

I encourage you to send out handwritten notes to first-time guests in your church. They need to receive a short letter saying "we are glad that you came." You may not realize it, but this note will be a determining factor in the guest's willingness to return to your church. If a handwritten note is all that stands in between a guest returning or not returning to my church, I will write the note every single time. Please tell your Pastor that he should write every note until he has more than 30 first-time families in a given week. It's important. And it will grow your church.

The other church-related handwritten note I encourage is the follow-up thank-you note. Each month at my Board meeting, I give out the list of repeat visitors who are not quite ready to join the church yet. I encourage my Board members to send out a card or expression of gratitude for the guest's visit. We have seen time and again where relationships are formed because of this communication that takes place between my church members and guests. Guests come from the fringe of the church to the point where they are ready to integrate into the life of our faith community fully. While it is not completely because of a handwritten note, the handwritten note goes a long, long way!

I challenge you to become a person of gratitude as you value the power of the handwritten note.

5) Consider a Handwritten Prayer Note

Prayer is always a blessing to someone else. A wise mentor gave me the greatest comfort of all in a difficult situation by saying, "We can pray." It was perhaps one of the most profound moments of my life. It became the foundation for me moving from a person who prays to becoming a person of prayer. He was exactly right. In those moments of life when it seems like there is nothing else we can do, we can pray!

Let me encourage you to be a person who sends a note from time to time not to tell people what they should do, but rather to offer up a prayer. How would you feel if someone else sent you a note simply to say, "I prayed for you today." For the vast majority of us, it might change our circumstance as we know that we are not alone. Such peace emerges in knowing that someone else is going to God on our behalf and that he unites with us in lifting up our need before God.

The problem is that we all have a "fix it" mentality. We want to fix it even more quickly than we want to lift it up to God. Psalm 46:10 (NIV) says, "Be still, and know that I am God."[139] It doesn't say for us to get busier. It says for us to be still. Stop. Quit moving. Allow God to be God. Send a handwritten note from time to time that simply says, "Friend, God loves you dearly and I am praying for you!"

6) Keep it Timely

---

[139] Psalm 46:10, (NIV)

Nothing is worse than when a situation is well in the past, and I've missed the momentum of God's perfect timing. Sometimes this happens when I am not informed of a ministry need that someone in my church has or it can be because we did not get out our handwritten notes in a timely fashion after the Sunday worship service. Handwritten notes are important, especially as we send them when someone is going through a life event or needs to be thanked for their generosity to us. Do not put off until tomorrow what you can accomplish today. Proverbs 6:4-11 (NLT) says, "Don't put it off; do it now! Don't rest until you do. Save yourself like a gazelle escaping from a hunter, like a bird fleeing from a net. Take a lesson from the ants, you lazybones. Learn from their ways and become wise! Though they have no prince or governor or ruler to make them work, they labor hard all summer, gathering food for the winter. But you, lazybones, how long will you sleep? When will you wake up? A little extra sleep, a little more slumber, a little folding of the hands to rest—then poverty will pounce on you like a bandit; scarcity will attack you like an armed robber."[140]   If we know of a need today, we should respond. It only takes a short time, and it can make all the difference in someone's life. A handwritten note may allow us to be Jesus to someone else.

How can these values inform your own note writing and help you to only write notes and posts that will build up the kingdom of God? (see Philippians 2:3-4)

_____

_____

_____

Dr. Chuck Lawless, Dean and Vice President of Graduate Studies and Ministries Centers at Southeastern Seminary in Wake

---

[140] Proverbs 6:4-11, (NLT)

Forest, NC offers the following as to why the handwritten note should make a revival:

1. It's thoughtful. Today, you can type a letter much faster than you can write it with a pen, not to mention that you can typically do it on your phone while you're walking down the street. A handwritten letter may not be as convenient, but it means more when you know someone has taken the time to sit down and write it out. In fact, I still have every note that has been written to me as far back as I can remember.
2. It's personal. Your handwriting will almost certainly have distinct differences from other people. Rather than using the Times New Roman font which 99% of the world seems to write in, you have a specific penmanship that will add your personal touch. I can actually see people in my mind when I read their notes and see their writing, and that image brings me great joy.
3. It's surprising. Writing a note by hand gives you the opportunity to surprise someone. I love leaving a note where the person can stumble across it. It's much more exciting to find a note on your car windshield than in your email inbox. It's even exciting when you receive that note in the old-fashioned mailbox.[141]

The Value of Journaling

Through the years, it has become much easier for me to write my thoughts down on paper. At the end of each day, I tell God about what happened during the day; I give God my joys and concerns. What I am learning is that the more I write, the more I can let go of what I am feeling to place it in God's hands. Rather than being weighted down by keeping a situation or life circumstance bottled up, God becomes my partner in sharing the

---

[141] Lawless, Chuck. "3 Reasons To Bring Back The Handwritten Note." ChuckLawless.com http://chucklawless.com/2016/10/3-reasons-to-bring-back-the-handwritten-note/ (accessed February 3, 2017).

load.

When journaling, I like to observe the following order:

First, I tell God what happened during the day. At the end of each paragraph (which also is usually the end of each event as well!), I say something like, "God, I pray for this circumstance that you would receive it and have me do with it what you will … both now and in the days to come." If I am struggling with a person or issue, I might say, "God, please help me to see this as you would have me to see it." Doing this helps me not only to celebrate the good elements of my life but also to let go of the challenges of each day.

Second, I give God praise and thanks for the day's events. God is always good; all the good that comes into my life comes from Him. We should always praise God because He is worthy of our praise and thank Him for his goodness.

Third, I try to think about the day to come. What will be my action items tomorrow, both new and as I finish up today's events? It helps me to start the day before it begins as I prepare for the day ahead.

Fourth, I put it all into the context of the Bible; this usually happens as I read a devotional with scripture. Let me caution you. Make sure that you read actual scripture and not just a devotion that is about scripture. I finish with prayer as I lift it all up to God. is simply conversation with my best friend, and God is my best friend.

Journaling for me is about writing a love letter to God. As I write my love notes to God, He gives me a peace of mind and calms my soul … a peace and calm that can come only by the power of the Holy Spirit.

Do you journal? Why or why not? How can you use journaling ot your benefit?

_____

_____

Start to write handwritten notes today; it's never too late!

RECEIVE PRAYER REQUESTS BEFORE JOINING IN
UNISON IN THE CLOSING PRAYER:

**Dear Lord, thank you for the written word... our Bible.
Thank you that sharing the written word has allowed
countless millions to come to faith in Jesus Christ through
the centuries. Show me how to be someone that values the
written word, both as a means of building up your kingdom
and others. Give me a love for handwritten notes and
journaling. In Jesus' name, AMEN.**

HOMEWORK: READ SESSION TWELVE AND WRITE
DOWN YOUR ANSWERS TO THE QUESTIONS FOR GROUP
DISCUSSION BEFORE THE NEXT GROUP SESSION

www.TheBlessedLifeBook.com

SECTION FOUR

The Blessing Challenge

SESSION TWELVE
It's Never Too Late
to Live the Blessed Life

OPEN THE BIBLE STUDY SESSION WITH PRAYER. ASK
GOD TO BLESS YOUR TIME TOGETHER.

ANSWER THE QUESTIONS FOR GROUP DISCUSSION
BELOW

My father used to say that it's never too late to do anything you
wanted to do. And he said, "You never know what you can
accomplish until you try."

Michael Jordan[142]

Most of us live our lives with regret. The regret of what
might have been sometimes outweighs our ability to find blessings
in the present. Either we live our lives looking in the rearview
mirror of what we should have done differently or we live life
looking to the future because we are convinced that the future will
magically be better.

A friend of mine once said that intentionality is the only thing that
separates someone who achieves much in life from those who
achieve little. Thinking about this, how can you be intentional
about accomplishing great things for the kingdom of God this
week?

_____

_____

---

[142] "Never Too Late." BrainyQuotes.com
https://www.brainyquote.com/quotes/quotes/m/michaeljor447180.html?src=t_never_too_lat
e (accessed February 3, 2017).

What area of your life to you need to let go of and give it to God?

_____

_____

_____

Consider this: many times we are bogged down because we do not do the tasks first that cause us to use the most energy. Those things that we dread doing often become stumbling blocks because they kill our creativity. Mark Twain once said, "If it's your job to eat a frog, it's best to do it first!" What frogs do you need to eat right now? (daily, weekly, monthly, yearly?)

_____

_____

_____

Live Life in the Present

The truth is that living in the past or the future is dangerous because it can rob us of present joy. God wants us to make each moment count as we live in the here and now.

Abraham was 75 years when he was called by God (Genesis 12:4). He then ministered for 100 years before his death at age 175 (Genesis 25:7). Jesus is one of the most well-known figures of all times, but he only ministered for three years as an adult (age 30-33). A beloved uncle in my family was given two months to live; he died over four years later. These stories are a reminder that we need to make each day count as we seek to do the very best that we can with today; do not worry so much about how much time you have left! As Morgan Freeman's character says in the movie *Shawshank Redemption*, "It's time either to get busy living or get busy dying." Choose life each day and in each moment you are alive!

Keep in mind that there is only so much time in the world. We need to guard our time. We cannot do everything. We have to determine what and who are most important to us. I like to prioritize my life in the following way. My daily relationship with God is first. The family is second. Friends are third. Everything else (including my work) comes below those top three priorities. It has become a litmus test that from time to time reminds me to get back to that which is most important to me.

What are your priorities in life?

_____

_____

_____

Does your checkbook and time agree with your order of priorities?

_____

_____

_____

Incredible Accomplishments In A Short Time

- Alexander the Great ascended to his father's throne at the age of 16. He conquered his first countries at the age of 18. He died at the age of 32.
- Joan of Arc was 17 when she became a French crusader. While she would die two years later at the age of 19, she is

still a household name.

- At the age of 12, Blaise Pascal was studying geometry. By the age of 19 (in 1642), he began to develop the first ever calculator.
- At the age of 5, Wolfgang Amadeus Mozart composed short pieces of music. By age 8, he wrote his first symphony. Mozart would die at the age of 32, but his music will be remembered forever.[143]

While countless other examples could be named, the point is the same in each case: Do what you can with today! Don't worry about yesterday or tomorrow. As the scriptures say in Matthew 6:34 (NIV), "Each day has enough trouble of its own."[144] Your experiences to this point in life make you who you are. Someone once asked me if I would change anything about my life. While I do have some regrets about certain situations where I could have done some life events differently, I would not change a anything. My wife and children are the most precious thing to me on this earth. If I were to change some of the factors of my past, I possibly could miss out on marrying a wife whom I love dearly or beautiful children who adore their dad (and whom I adore!). My future is in God's hands. The one bit of advice that I give you is to grow where you are planted.

Do you have regrets about your past? In what areas of your life would it beneficial to let go of the past and focus on your present and future?

_____

_____

_____

---

[143] Cain, Aine. "17 People Who Accomplished Incredible Things At An Incredibly Young Age." BusinessInsider.com http://www.businessinsider.com/people-who-accomplished-incredible-things-young-2017-1/#alexander-the-great-conquered-countries-at-18-1 (accessed February 3, 2017).

[144] Matthew 6:34, (NIV)

Bobby Bowden was asked about the ideal coaching job. Bobby said that he wanted to make the place where he was currently coaching the absolute best job that he could imagine. He retired with two National Championships to show for himself. That's how I feel about my ministry. I am called by God to be in ministry, yes. I am also called by God to grow where I am planted. Instead of constantly looking for the next church, God wants me to do my very best where I am currently in ministry. He wants me to grow the church and to grow the body of believers in what it means to know Jesus Christ as their Lord and Savior.[145]

How can you grow where you are planted? How would growing where you are planted be a benefit to you?

_____

_____

_____

As we live life in the present and realize that God can accomplish much through us in a short period of time, it is never too late to live the blessed life!

THE GREATEST BLESSING

The Following is An Ivitation to Follow Jesus Christ

Do you want to know Jesus as Your Lord and Savior?

Do you yearn to experience the Lord's comforting presence, power, and wisdom? That's good, because God loves you and wants to have a personal relationship with you forever.

---

[145] Bobby Bowden gave a television interview to WCTV news when I was a child. While paraphrased, his words continue to impact my life into the present day.

The problem is . . . one thing separates you from a relationship with God—sin. You and I sin whenever we fail to live by the Lord's holy standard. In fact, Romans 3:23 (NIV): "All have sinned and fall short of the glory of God."[146]

Furthermore, Romans 6:23 explains that the penalty for sin is death—separation from God in hell forever. No matter how hard we try, we cannot save ourselves or get rid of our sins. We can't earn our way to heaven by being good, going to church, or being baptized (Eph. 2:8-9).

Understanding how helpless we are because of our sins, God sent His only Son, Jesus, to save us.

Jesus Christ lived a perfect, sinless life, and then died on the cross to pay the penalty for our sins (Rom. 5:8). Three days later, He rose from the dead—showing that He had triumphed over sin and death once and for all.

So how can you know God?

It all starts with accepting Jesus Christ as your Lord and Savior. Jesus Christ provides a relationship with the Father and eternal life through His death on the cross and resurrection (Rom. 5:10).

Romans 10:9 promises, "If you confess with your mouth Jesus as Lord, and believe in your heart that God raised Him from the dead, you will be saved." If you have not yet begun your personal relationship with God, understand that the One who created you loves you no matter who you are or what you've done. He wants you to experience the profound depth of His care.

Therefore, tell God that you are willing to trust Him for salvation. You can tell Him in your own words or use this simple prayer:

"Lord Jesus, I ask You to forgive my sins and save me from eternal separation from God. By faith, I accept Your work and death on the cross as sufficient payment for my sins. Thank You for

---

[146] Romans 3:23, (NIV)

providing the way for me to know You and to have a relationship with my heavenly Father. Through faith in You, I have eternal life. Thank You also for hearing my prayers and loving me unconditionally. Please give me the strength, wisdom, and determination to walk in the center of Your will. In Jesus' name, amen."

If you have just prayed this prayer, congratulations!

You have received Christ as your Savior and have made the best decision you will ever make—one that will change your life forever! Please let your Pastor know. Also, please let us know by emailing us at decision@theblessedlifebook.com so we can rejoice with you and pray for you.[147]

RECEIVE PRAYER REQUESTS AND JOIN TOGETHER IN UNISON IN THE CLOSING PRAYER

Dear Lord, we all know regret… regret of missing an important opportunity or regret in a human relationship. Free us from regret as we let go of our past and live in the present. Help us to look forward to the blessings you have in store for our future. We pray for your blessings to reign down upon us and those around us. We claim your blessings as we live for you each day. Most of all, we are grateful for the blessing of Jesus Christ and how He died on the cross for our sins so long ago. Today, we commit our lives to you and living for Jesus everyday. In Jesus' name, AMEN.

www.TheBlessedLifeBook.com

---

[147] Stanley, Charles. "How Do I Accept Jesus As My Savior?" InTouch.org https://www.intouch.org/read/content/how-do-i-accept-jesus-as-my-savior (accessed February 8, 2017)

www.ingramcontent.com/pod-product-compliance
Lightning Source LLC
Chambersburg PA
CBHW072009040426
42447CB00009B/1553